What You Give

Kate Erion

ARCHWAY
PUBLISHING

Archway Publishing books may be ordered through booksellers or by contacting:

Archway Publishing
1663 Liberty Drive
Bloomington, IN 47403
www.archwaypublishing.com
844-669-3957

ISBN: 978-1-6657-5787-4 (sc)
ISBN: 978-1-6657-5788-1 (e)

Library of Congress Control Number: 2024904617

Print information available on the last page.

Archway Publishing rev. date: 03/11/2024

For All Parents Everywhere

PART I

"All That's Gone Before"

The Nap

I hear hurricanes a-blowing
I know the end is coming soon
I fear rivers overflowing
I hear the voice of rage and ruin

From *Bad Moon Rising* by John Fogerty

We whispered about a worrisome matter. Dressed only in our underwear, we lay dutifully between the clean, pressed cotton sheets in the double bed we shared. On a wide-awake winter afternoon in 1953 when my sister Carlyn and I were supposed to be napping, sunshine streamed through the foundation windows at the top of our painted concrete block bedroom walls. We were concerned that this house did not have a fireplace. Yet every book that had ever been read to us clearly stated that Santa Claus enters homes through their fireplaces. If he came down our chimney, we feared it would be to his peril.

The furnace room was right off our basement bedroom, so we crept out of bed and tiptoed across the cold linoleum to assess the situation. Opening the door to the unpainted dark gray room, we felt the radiant heat and heard the rumbling of the burning fuel. We puzzled about which duct was the chimney, yet all the ducts attached to the furnace were so narrow even a child could see that a fat man wouldn't pass through them. We stared with alarm at the pulsating orange glow in the window of the furnace's tiny iron door. This was a disaster waiting to happen!

Mom called down the stairs that we had better be in bed. We dashed back into our room, crawled between the sheets and resumed our hushed discussion about Santa. Was Santa allowed to come in through the front door? Would he come at all? Should we try to get a message to him? How would we go about that?

1

We heard Mom's stern voice again from upstairs.

"Go to sleep!"

Carlyn and I looked at each other in astonishment.

"How can she hear us?" we puzzled.

Staring up at the rough-textured ceiling it looked obvious to me. In the white plaster there were tiny bubble holes that I supposed went all the way through the ceiling to the living room floor above it. I stood up in bed to point out the miniscule holes to my sister.

"She can hear us through these," I said.

"I told you girls to go to sleep."

Mom's angry voice just at the top of the stairs startled me. I lay back down and tried, really, not to talk anymore. But eventually, one of us thought about the Metzers next door, and we were whispering again. The Metzer family didn't have a fireplace either, one of us pointed out. Furthermore, there were more kids in their family. Santa wouldn't deny gifts to a family of six. And those very kids had told us confidently that Santa was coming to their house. Certainly, one of us asked the other, Santa would come to our house, too, wouldn't he?

A terrifying crescendo of heavy feet descending the wooden stairs stopped our discussion. Mom barged into our room drilling us with pinched eyes as she grabbed a paddle-ball paddle off our dresser. Panicked by her malevolent expression we started to scream. She rolled us over, first one, then the other, and with white knuckles lifted the paddle high in the air. As the wooden paddle cracked down, we screamed in pain and fear. The stinging smacks burned our bottoms red as we begged her to stop, but Mom did not relent until she had delivered five smacks apiece. She left us crying with a stern warning that we had better sleep, or she would be back. She left the paddle on the dresser and went upstairs.

Sleep now was out of the question. After the tears we began to discuss in urgent whispers how to protect ourselves from another attack. Paradoxically, lying silently in bed never occurred to us. What was clear to me, though, was that if we were to remove the weapon no one would get hurt. But Carlyn understood what I did not: there would be consequences.

"No!" she advised.

Regardless, I tip-toed out of bed, removed the paddle from the dresser top and tucked it behind a bookcase that stood against the wall. Although Carlyn was not in favor of subterfuge, neither was she willing to put the paddle back where it had been. As we continued to argue through the pros and cons of this strategy, Mom's feet boomed down the steps again. I froze for one panicky moment, but confidence returned the instant I reminded myself the paddle was well hidden. We would get through this unharmed. Mom charged into the room and reached out for the paddle. Her eyes widened, then narrowed and pinned us.

"Which one of you took it?"

I would not talk. I would not tell. She could hang a light bulb over my head and interrogate me Dick Tracy-style, but I would not open my mouth.

"Tell me what you did with it!" hollered Mom as she stalked the bed.

Carlyn caved with a sob, got out of bed and retrieved the paddle from behind the bookcase. With her head hanging low she delivered the paddle penitently to Mom.

I shrieked at Carlyn from the bed, "No! No! No!"

Mom flipped us over, one at a time, and spanked us both with righteous authority, returned the paddle to the dresser and stomped back up the stairs.

Astounded by my sister's betrayal, I demanded an explanation.

"What did you DO that for?! Why did you give her the paddle?!"

In my astonishment I forgot to modulate my volume. Carlyn was more upset that we had conspired against Mom than about the spanking.

"Mommy asked us to give the paddle back," my sister said between sobs.

Interrupted for the third dreadful time we heard Mom's feet thundering down the stairs. Then we heard a heavy thud, a moan and silence. The expression on my face must have been as if Santa Claus had just emerged hale and hearty from the furnace room.

"Is she dead?" I asked with hope in my voice.

The word "dead" had a different effect on Carlyn. She leapt up and ran out to the foot of the stairs, screaming.

"Mommy! Mommy! Mommy!"

I remained in bed holding my breath and listening.

"Get back in bed!" Mom shouted her order at Carlyn.

I felt betrayed by the Universe when I heard Mom's snarling voice. I wondered, not in the tone of sarcasm a teenager might use, but in the awed tone of a child who believed a witch could disguise herself as my mother, "Who IS this woman and what has she done with Mommy?"

As my sister crawled back into bed and stifled her sobs in her pillow, I heard Mom groan and the stairs creak as she pulled her bruised but unbroken body up. She finally had the silence she demanded.

∼

Who is this Woman?

Hunger, I discovered, is very much a matter of the mind, and as I began to study my own appetites, I saw that my teenage craving had not really been for food. That ravenous desire had been a yearning for love, attention, appreciation. Food had merely been my substitute.

Ruth Reichl, chef, cook-book author, co-producer
of PBS's *Gourmet's Diary of a Foodie*

Somewhere in the mess that is my office there is a black and white photograph of Ruth Stern, my mom, lined up with four of her siblings. Grandma Stern in the back holds a baby, who must be Uncle Paul. The photo was taken in the early 1930s when Mom would have been 12 or 13 years old. She is as lovely in that photo as a lean, young Calvin Klein model. She stands in the sunshine outside the family's two-story, white-washed farmhouse wearing a loosely fitting cotton dress. Her long, wavy hair is darker than blonde, but sun-kissed enough to look auburn. There is a light dusting of freckles across her fair face. Although the sunshine is in her brown eyes, they sparkle, and her grin says she enjoys this photo opportunity. She looks smart, confident and athletic. She looks like a girl with spunk and promise. She looks like someone who could have been my best friend.

Sometimes on gray winter afternoons Mom sat between my sister and me on the couch reading Robert Louis Stevenson's poems from *A Child's Garden of Verses* (Stevenson)[1] or telling us stories from her own life. One of the stories she told was of galloping her dad's tall plow horse alone and bareback across the South Dakota grassland. If the horse stumbled in a prairie dog hole and threw her to the ground, she would have to lead him to a fence to remount him. The challenge was that a fence might be miles away. So, yes, she had pluck.

Ruth was not a child of privilege. Her father was a rural minister for the Church of the Brethren. For most of her childhood in the 1920s and 1930s Church of the Brethren pastors did not receive a salary. Their Church provided their clergy with farmland and a house (a relative term - one congregation put the Stern family up in a chicken coop), and that was all.

Their name said it all. The Sterns worked hard; they prayed hard; then they went back to work.

Every one of the Stern kids, except Mom, graduated from college - which I think is exceptional given their economic circumstances. Mom enrolled in Bemidji State Teachers College, but in her sophomore year in 1940 while Europe was at war, she quit school and moved to Chicago. Her first job was as an au pair for a wealthy family in Chicago's affluent Lincoln Park neighborhood. She didn't work there long before she took a job as a telephone operator, but I wonder what her relationship was like with the family's children while she was employed there. Mom was adamant with us that she would never tolerate "whiney", and she would never "spoil" us with softness. She was true to her word.

She wouldn't have been the only parent in those years with such a moral philosophy, but it is curious to me that in 1945, before Mom was married, pediatrician Dr. Benjamin Spock published a best seller called *Baby and Childcare* (Spock)[2] that rocked the world. Spock had a radical idea: be affectionate with your children and try to understand their individual needs! I'd be astounded if Mom ever read that book, but hear of it she must have, because Spock was a leading authority on children's needs. In fact, his book is still in print today. I would not be surprised to learn that without having read the book Mom discounted Spock's ideas as mind-addling permissiveness. Perhaps, she was jealously reluctant to give something she herself had been deprived of. Her family wasn't unkind, but they were frugal with their affection. It could be they believed praise was reserved for God alone.

Mom was a middle child. As such she didn't stand a chance to get attention in a family of six kids while her mother was baking bread, washing, ironing, mending, chopping wood, feeding chickens, weeding the garden, cleaning house, and changing the baby. In her spare time Grandma tended to parishioners who were needy, sick, or giving birth. A middle child would have to do something astounding to call attention to herself if she were ever to be noticed by such a busy mother.

Mom's only sister Martha was six years older than Mom. In that photo in my office Aunt Martha looks like a cool beauty with her dark hair pulled back from her contemplative face. She was, in fact, the first-born child. Grandma had six years to bond with her while boys were born. She wanted Martha to study art because of her remarkable talent at drawing, but by the time Martha was grown she had caught the missionary bug. After nursing school, away she went to Lima, Peru where she worked as a surgery nurse.

Whatever Aunt Martha could do that met with Grandma's acclaim, Mom would do, too, but bigger and without the approbation. If Aunt Martha planted a flower garden, Mom would plant a grander garden with rocks she levered into it to create a multi-textured, multi-dimensional garden.

And then later, to Mom's advantage, there was one thing that Aunt Martha could not do. She could not have children. Mom might have been a little smug announcing her first pregnancy to her mother three months after she and Dad married.

In my adult years one of Mom's brothers who grew up to be a career alcoholic (if you have to be one, give it your all!), told me with the confidence of an expert in his field that all his siblings were alcoholics. I can't say whether he was correct, but wouldn't it be astounding if it were true? Grandpa and Grandma believed in abstinence from alcohol. Actually, they believed in abstinence from everything a person might enjoy too much. No dancing, no smoking, no wearing bright colors, no jewelry, no make-up. I wonder whether they even disparaged laughter. The list went on, so there is no doubt that neither one of them ever tasted a single drop of liquor in their entire lives. They admonished their children and their parishioners also to go with the Temperance Union and "buy dry".

As an adult Mom certainly enjoyed her cocktails, I'll give my uncle that much. There was no Weight Watcher menu she did not alter to include a libation, although carefully limiting her choice of mix to water so as not to add a calorie. It always looked to me, though, that her real source of comfort was food.

Mom struggled with her weight because Dad wanted his wife to be a "credit" to him. Of course, a plump wife could never do that, because he didn't recognize any virtue in a woman thick through the waist. It must not have occurred to Mom that a man who demands an elegant woman to enhance his value doesn't believe in his own merit. Mom may have had self-doubts of her own that motivated her to go along with Dad's conditional love. I remember every time Mom stepped off the bathroom scale, she swore that simply smelling food added pounds.

Dad had choice remarks to sling at her in those instances.

"By morning I'll be sober, but you'll still be fat!"

Mom hated herself, ate to feel better, then hated herself more than ever.

When Grandma died in the 1970s all of us convened at Grandma and Grandpa's home in Franklin Grove, Illinois. A few of us children and grandchildren gathered in our grandparents' parlor to catch up with each other on mundane matters as families do who live great distances apart. Someone brought up that the date was close to Grandma's birthday.

"That would make Grandma a Cancer," I said, always looking for clues to help explain what makes each of us tick.

Grandpa Stern stepped into the parlor as I made this remark. He was not a fan of horoscopes.

"That is blasphemy!" said Grandpa in his authoritative preacher's voice.

His grief quickly ignited. His preacher eyes flashed lightning bolts.

"Horoscopes are bunk!"

I blushed scarlet at this public redress as he crossed the room to sit on the loveseat next to Uncle Dave.

My uncle moved over to make space for him during the awkward silence while I bled out. With a merry look on his face Uncle Dave took it upon himself to break the silence, saying something like:

"You put horoscopes in the same category as you put Charles Darwin."

Like a flash of lightning, Grandpa smacked his cane against the floor in a giggle-stopping strike.

"Don't you ever speak that man's name in my house again!" he commanded.

Later my uncle divulged that sometime during her twenties while Mom lived in Chicago, she took it upon herself to send a copy of Charles Darwin's *Origin of the Species* (Darwin)[3] to her fundamentalist father. She had to have known it would not be a gift well-received. Was she sharing an alternative point of view in hopes that she and he might have an enlightening discussion about evolution? Mom respected her father, but nevertheless, the woman I knew intended to goad him. Negative attention is still attention.

~

Nash

"You are a man, not God; you are human, not an angel. How can you expect to remain always in a constant state of virtue, when this was not possible even for an angel of Heaven, nor for the first man in the Garden?"

Thomas à Kempis

Grandma sat between my cousin Jeanie and me in the backseat of Grandpa's early1950s baby blue Nash. We cousins were a year apart in age and I believe we were eleven and twelve years old at that time. Grandma didn't mind riding in the back seat with us. She screamed less there. I wasn't sure if it was Grandpa's driving, or that a car traveled faster than a horse and buggy, but Grandma never was at ease in a car. I had heard of her kneeling as she held her folded hands over the back seat while she prayed aloud for God to bring her family safely to their destination. There was nothing that could be said to Grandma to give her reassurance. As a child I could only bear witness of Grandma's terror-stricken face and Grandpa's taut jaw muscles while his white knuckles clutched the steering wheel.

But this was a clear, sunny Sunday. Traffic was light as we puttered down the Franklin Grove, Illinois residential street at 25 MPH. We were headed to Dixon to return Jeanie home to Uncle Bill who had allowed her to sleep overnight with my sister and me while we visited our grandparents. Carlyn had the front passenger seat where she could listen for the ticking turn signal that Grandpa couldn't hear. It was her job to tell him when to turn it off.

The Nash passed a Craftsman style home where a smiling man stood on a step ladder painting his front porch the color of rich cream. He looked pleased to have a fine-weather day for his chore, but he exhibited more joy than a modest reason could provide. His smile spread clear across his face. His lips were parted as if he were laughing. You can't see something like that and not smile in reaction. As a light breeze blew over me where I sat by the open car window, I speculated. Had he just heard a funny joke? Had he just bought his first house? Had he just married? Had he just found out he was going to be a father?

"There must be a dire emergency that he has to paint on the Lord's Day," said Grandma in a quiet but disapproving tone.

My reflexive smile waned as I turned to look at her. She stared straight ahead, her chin a little higher than usual, her lips pressed into a straight line. Jeanie watched out the window on her side of the car. As Grandpa's co-pilot, Carlyn watched the street ahead. Grandpa hadn't heard the remark. No one commented.

Ah, the fourth commandment was the thought that came to my mind. "Remember the Sabbath day to keep it holy ... In it you shall do no work ..." [4] (The Holy Bible)

The painter looked neither guilty nor ashamed. He could not have cared less that he was breaking someone's commandment.

As I understand it, Grandma's birth family had been more relaxed in their adherence to biblical tenets. Grandma's rigidity developed after she was fostered to the Wolf family when her beloved father, William Barkley, died. The Barkley's had just moved from Pennsylvania to Illinois for the promise of opportunity they did not have in Pennsylvania. Great Grandpa had hired on at a productive farm near Dixon, Illinois. He might have aspired to buy his own farm one day in the fertile Midwest if he worked hard enough. And he would have to work harder than the average man because Great Grandpa had lost an arm in a mill accident years earlier. Lifting hay onto a wagon with one arm in a sunny field on a muggy June day might have been his undoing. He collapsed and died from apparent heat stroke in that field. All the family's relatives lived out east. There was no family close enough to help out - only strangers to support the grieving widow and her five young children. Each child was fostered into a separate family who said they could offer a bed to sleep in and a meal, but there was no free charity. Every farm needed laborers. Only the baby got to stay with Grandma's mother who took in work as a laundress to support the two of them. The Christian farmer and his wife who took

Grandma put her to work washing dishes and baking bread. Did they believe that tribulation was God's punishment for sin? Did they explain Grandma's father's death and the dissolution of her family as such to her? Was it punishment? Did they teach her that salvation was achievable only through perfect adherence to The Ten Commandments? As an adult did Grandma feel resentful when she saw people break those Christian Commandments without retribution?

The answers to these questions could help me understand how Grandma Stern raised her children. I chuckle at the image of Grandma praying in the back seat of the car until I think about the trauma that an eight-year-old is put through when she loses her entire family. Therapy and social services weren't options at the turn of the 20th Century. Religion was all she was offered. As comforting as that might have been, when, as an adult, one of her babies died, the impact of that loss resulted in what her living children referred to as a "mental breakdown". And if it is true that her foster parents taught her that loss is punishment, did that result in her obsession with strict adherence to the Commandments? Uncle Paul told me that his mother whipped him soundly with a belt when she believed he had sinned.

~

The Introduction

Through this open world I'm a-bound to ramble
Through ice and snow, sleet and rain
I'm a-bound to ride that morning' railroad
Perhaps I'll die upon that train

From *Man of Constant Sorrow* by Bob Dylan

Bundled in a snowsuit Mom helped me put on, I waddled out the door to await the taxi. The sun hadn't come over the horizon yet. The neighborhood was in shadow. The sub-zero morning air burned my face, but I was not deterred. Even at three years old I accepted the northern Minnesota winter for what it was. Besides, I was on a meet and greet mission.

Now, before you say, "No one would allow a three-year-old child outdoors alone in the dark in sub-zero temperatures," you have to realize that in the early 1950s most American adults only recognized threats from outside the country. For the most part, it never occurred to them that dangers could exist in their own neighborhoods.

I was almost to the street when a black cab pulled up, its wheels squeaking on the snow. A cloud of smelly exhaust concealed the driver when he stepped out to open the trunk. A tall man wearing a long cloth coat stepped out of the passenger's rear door and placed a fedora neatly on his head. The clap of the trunk closing snapped sharply in the bitter cold. The driver reappeared and handed the man a suitcase. The man took something from his coat pocket and gave it to the driver.

I stared up at this lean man who had the posture of a soldier. Even at my age I knew what soldiers looked like. There were pictures in our albums of Daddy, Uncle Earl, Uncle Forrest, Uncle Dave, and Uncle Paul all wearing military uniforms.

As the sun rose, the man looked at me, said a dignified, "Hello," and then looked toward my house.

I said nothing although I knew who this stranger was. It had been nine months since I saw him last, but I heard about him every day. As the taxi pulled away the man squared his shoulders. He didn't reach out to take my hand. I didn't expect him to. I didn't have a lot of experience to draw from, after all. I didn't know then that some daddies might squat down and ask if the little daughter they hadn't seen in months was warm enough to be outside in this weather. Some daddies might call their daughter by name or ask which of his two daughters she was. Others might say, "My, how you have grown!" I accepted what was not given without judgment.

The man spent a second appraising my tiny home in the early morning sunshine. White vapor came from the chimney that jutted out of the flat, snow-covered roof. A picture window looked over my snow-filled yard. It was a humble one-bedroom house with both the bathroom and my bedroom in the basement, yet it was my world. I knew no other. The man's chin lifted slightly. And then he went striding up the driveway, each of his long steps squeaking on the frozen ground. He opened my frosted front door that also squeaked and went inside without knocking. What!?

I trotted after him to see how Mom was going to react to that. She met the man at the door wearing a smile covered in bright red Avon lipstick. This was the lipstick from the grown-up's tube, and not the lipstick from the tiny sample tubes my sister and I always looked for in Mom's Avon Lady satchel. She had on her church dress instead of her usual house dress. The night before she had pinned up her dark brown hair with bobby pins so this morning it curled stylishly.

The man removed his hat revealing crew cut hair as black as the fur of a Labrador Retriever. His long face looked ruddy from the cold. The outer corners of his eyes tilted slightly downward. It startled me to see him take off his coat and hang it in the front closet - as if it were his closet to use.

Mom said, "Say hello to your daddy, Kathy."

I looked up into this man's blue eyes. He met my gaze but said nothing directly to me. I said nothing back.

"Can you give your daddy a hug?" encouraged my mother with a gentle nudge.

I locked my knees and pushed back.

Daddy had just arrived from "up" in Thule, Greenland. He was a lot like God who lived "up" in heaven. You never saw Him, but you were told daily what He wanted or what He expected of your behavior. My sister Carlyn and I thought of Greenland and heaven as one and the same, or at least as neighboring countries. In fact, once when Mom, Carlyn and I were on the Bemidji city bus we rode past a cemetery. Being a worldly four-year old, my sister knew that people who went to the cemetery were said to be "up in heaven".

Looking out the bus window Carlyn said in a conversational voice that carried to the other passengers, "That's where Daddy is."

Strangers in this post-war world gave us sympathetic looks. Mom, a chatty extrovert, was momentarily stunned into silence.

It took her a couple of seconds to respond, purposely loud enough to inform the other passengers, "No, Honey. Daddy works in Greenland!"

The remaining details of the morning Dad returned home are foggy, but there were no hugs. Dad did not draw us onto his lap or tell us how glad he was to see us. He did not tell us he missed us. Dad probably said something like, "It's not any warmer here than in Thule."

And I imagine Mom would have laughed at a joke like that in her relief that Dad was back home without a hitch. There was a reason for her to be relieved, I learned decades later from an uncle.

The discharged Army personnel who helped build an American Air Force base in Greenland in the early 1950s served under a strictly enforced no alcohol policy. Dad served three terms in Thule, and on at least one trip home to Bemidji after the standard nine-month stint was finished, Dad's return was delayed a day or two by partying that probably began as soon as the furloughed men were wheels up off that island and continued after touching down in New York. Dad went incommunicado. Not on purpose. It's just that, as I was to learn much later, it is hard for a black-out drunk to remember to call home. Mom had paced the floor with great concern, but in those days, all she could do was wait for him to call her. I can only imagine that one end of such a phone call was sheepish, and the other end was fraught with exasperated incredulity.

~

Bloody Nose

The baby laughs a lot
And that's the most important thing

From *Myths* by Joan Baez

Early one winter evening when supper was ready, Mom called my sister and me to the kitchen, where our little wooden table was set for four. A ceiling lamp hung low over the center of the table. It cast a circle of light over the three of us in the otherwise unlit house. From the kitchen we could see the dark sky through the south-facing picture window. A narrow streak of orange light on the horizon shrunk rapidly.

I slid onto a smooth, heavy wooden chair that raised me high enough so my nose was level with the tabletop. Carlyn sat down across from me and asked where Daddy was. Mom glanced toward the window and said we weren't going to wait for him any longer. She poured milk into our glasses. When I reached up for my milk my grasp wasn't secure. The glass went over with a clunk. As milk flooded across the tablecloth, a wallop across my face slung me to the floor. The chair clattered over on top of me. Milk and blood dripped on the linoleum.

Mom yelled, "Look what you've done!"

I touched my throbbing nose, and my fingers came away red. I felt a hysterical sob forming in my throat.

As the sob began to rise, my mother's voice warned, "No crying! Go lie down on the couch!"

Obediently I crossed to the houndstooth couch under the picture window and lay down without making a sound. I believed when Dad got home, he would tell me that he was sorry for my bloody nose. He would lay his hand on my forehead, and I would be redeemed. Minutes ticked by. Mom sputtered herself silent as she wiped the table, the floor and changed the tablecloth. By the time the front door opened the only sound was the clink of my sister's fork on her plate. Dad stepped into the dim entryway. Hope flowed into me. I watched him remove his jacket and over-boots and start across the living room toward the kitchen. When he saw me in the shadows, he paused but did not approach.

"What are you doing on the couch?"

"I got a bloody nose," I said, anticipating his tender touch.

Mom immediately interrupted, "Supper is getting cold."

Chastened like someone who already knew he was guilty, Dad went on into the kitchen and sat down at his place at the table. Mom excused my sister who went downstairs. I lay silently in the dim light waiting.

My parents' voices were quiet, but I heard Mom ask, "Where were you?"

Dad had had a beer with his boss Kelly at the body shop, he told Mom while she flicked a scoop of mashed potatoes on his plate. Their talk was quiet and stilted. It didn't interest me. I lay still and waited. After a while I heard my name.

"Kathy, go downstairs," Mom said.

I sat up and looked at my parents. There was unfinished business. I got up and walked slowly across the living room to the top of the stairs, but lingered there, waiting. I looked back at them. Mom watched Dad. Dad watched his plate. Then Mom's eyes turned on me.

"Downstairs. Now."

Quickly I ducked down the steps as I tried to comprehend what had happened. In our bedroom my sister sat cross-legged on our bed and dressed her doll.

I stood in front of her on the gray squares of linoleum and reminded her, "I got a bloody nose."

"You tipped over your milk," she said.

She already grasped that every action is followed by a consequence. No one ever mentioned the incident again. In fact, as I look back across that memory, I doubt that Mom ever told Dad what she had done. I doubt also that he ever thought to ask how I had come to have a bloody nose.

Mikey

Beware the wound becomes the knife.

Paraphrased from *If You Meet the Buddha on
The Road, Kill Him!* by Sheldon B Kopp

Carlyn started kindergarten that fall. It felt lonely to be without her on weekday mornings. The neighbors who lived in the lot west of us, the Pages, had a son Mikey who, like me, didn't go to school. After Mom hung up from the phone call inviting Mrs. Metzer and her daughter Marilyn for coffee that morning, Mom and I walked across the dew-covered grass to invite Mrs. Page and Mikey to come for coffee, too. Mom explained to me about Mikey.

"He is a Mongoloid Idiot," she said using the vernacular of the day.

No one had heard of a "syndrome" in those days.

"What's a Mongoloid Idiot?" I asked.

"That means he's retarded," she clarified.

My next question had to be "What's 'retarded'?" Pre-schoolers in 1954 were not as worldly as today's preschoolers. Mom smiled an indecipherable smile. "It means he's dumb", she said. Ah, thought I. I know what dumb is. Stupid. Fool. Idiot.

Mrs. Page invited us into her tidy little home. Mom and Mrs. Page settled into easy chairs in the living room for a conversation while I remained standing near the door, not knowing what to do with myself. Then Mikey entered the living room. He was a round-headed child about my height with closely cropped blonde hair. He didn't look at me or speak. I didn't speak to him, either, but I stared at him intently, this "dumb" boy with his bumpy tongue hanging from his mouth. Mom and Mrs. Page talked about him in front of us, like all adults did with all kids, like we were all dumb. She would have to send him away if she were to put him

19

in school, said Mrs. Page. She looked out the window as she spoke, like she was trying to see down the future. But yes, she and Mikey would enjoy coming for coffee.

An hour later Mrs. Metzer, her three-year-old daughter Marilyn, Mrs. Page and Mikey converged at our front door. Once the ladies were seated at the kitchen table with their cups of coffee, we kids were urged to "Go play." I was at a loss. I wasn't used to the role of leader. That was my sister's job. What do you do with a three-year old and a silent, dumb boy, I wondered, with the superiority of a now four-year-old. They followed me around the house, watching everything I did. I took them outside to see my albino rabbit, Pinky Wiggles. Pinky wouldn't show himself. He stayed in the security of the shelter built into one end of the hutch.

We went back into the house. I gave them a tour. The room off the living room was my parents' bedroom. Mom had left a wire hanger lying on their bed. I picked up that hanger to put it back in the closet, but suddenly I turned and brought the hanger down on top of Mikey's head as hard as I could. He didn't make a sound, so I brought the hanger down hard again. Marilyn's eyes widened in shock, but she said nothing.

I told her in way of explanation, "He's dumb". I brought the hanger down on him a third time to show her that he was too dumb to even move away or cry or ask me to stop. Marilyn looked like she was going to cry, so I put the hanger in the closet and the three of us continued our tour of the house. Marilyn went silent, like the speechless Mikey. Now that I am an old woman what I did horrifies me, and it breaks my heart that those two little ones were willing to continue to follow me.

Not a quarter of an hour after the neighbors went home, Mom got a phone call from Mrs. Metzer. When Mom hung up the phone, she squatted down in front of me. She asked if I had hit Mikey with a hanger. Marilyn! Mom seemed more astonished than angry, but I was in a precarious situation. The less said, the better.

"He's dumb", was my only defense.

"Honey, you can't hit someone just because they're dumb," she told me with a hint of bewilderment.

I stared at her, trying to make sense of her words, her expression. It was puzzling. So, let me get this straight. You can hit someone if they are dumb AND mean, or dumb AND rude? I backed away in mistrust, and she let me go with no additional explanation.

In my four-year-old mind I gathered from listening to Mom and Mrs. Page that Mikey was not the way he was "supposed to be". Every time I wasn't the way I was "supposed to be" I was punished. I saw my action simply as giving Mikey what he deserved – what all imperfect children deserved.

~

Piano Lessons

Love is an expression and assertion of self-esteem,
a response to one's own value in the person of another.

Ayn Rand

When I turned four, I received a Golden Book called "The Littlest Ballerina" as a birthday gift. It contained full-page color drawings of a perfect little, red-headed girl who hoped to become a ballerina. Her hair was long and lovely. The artist had drawn individual lines depicting graceful locks that flowed over the girl's shoulders. Somehow this child was given magic dancing slippers that taught her how to point her feet in a plié. As she practiced, the shoes taught her more and more complicated steps until the girl was ready for her debut on stage. But when the time arrived for the performance, she couldn't find her magic dancing shoes anywhere. She had to borrow someone else's shoes for the performance. When she put on the loaned shoes, she remembered from her many hours of practice in the magic shoes, the proper way to move her feet. Her performance was a success. Voila! Through her hard work she had become a ballerina no longer in need of magic slippers.

Mom must have read that book to me dozens of times because, even though I couldn't read, I knew every word. I could turn the pages of the richly illustrated book in my lap and tell the entire story. When I was done "reading", I would fasten a pair of long-legged red pajama bottoms over my towheaded hair, and with the pajama legs dangling down my back like the tresses I imagined, I would dance around the sun-filled living room. I had discovered my heart's desire: to be a pretty ballerina. Note: not just a ballerina, but a pretty one with long hair.

As I danced my sister would sing along to Tennessee Ernie Ford's 45 rpm record "The Ballad of Davy Crockett"[5] (Blackburn) on our phonograph. A pediatrician had recommended that Mom encourage my tone-deaf sister to sing with records to help improve her pitch. It didn't seem to be effective. Even with the waistband of the pajamas tight over my ears I could hear sounds unbefitting my beautiful ballet. But compared to nothing it was the best background music I had, so on I danced.

"Born on a mountain in Tennessee" (twirl), "the greenest state in the land of the free" (stretch right), "raised in the woods so's he knew every tree" (stretch left), "he killed him a 'bar' when he was only three" (plié), "Davy, Davy Crockett, King of the Wild Frontier!" (En L'Air, extend and bow).

Once Dad was home from Greenland for good, he enrolled in Bemidji State Teachers College on the GI Bill. While there, a friend told him that the Minnesota Highway Patrol was expanding and was amenable to hiring honorably discharged service men. As a Bronze Star Medal recipient for heroic actions during the Battle of the Bulge in 1945, Dad's resume was impeccable. He applied and was hired. In the spring of 1954, he went away to Highway Patrol School, and in 1955 he was hired and stationed some 300 miles south of Bemidji in the tiny town of Spring Valley, just a few miles north of the Iowa line.

Although none of Minnesota's 10,000 lakes is in the southeast corner of Minnesota, there is an abundance of lesser-known rivers and creeks that trickle down to the Mighty one. The broad plains of the Midwest also roll down to meet the Mississippi River in this region. Spring Valley is a small farming community 150 miles give or take west of the Mississippi. This is the town where I started kindergarten, where I completed twelve grades of public school and where I dutifully endured eleven years of piano lessons.

Dad was a meticulous man. Mom steam pressed his shirts. His trousers were always perfectly creased. He kept his shoes impeccably shined and his nails carefully trimmed and clean. Every so often he pushed back his cuticles with an Emery stick. He said since he decided Carlyn and I were going to learn to play the piano, we would have to learn to groom our hands like he did. He asked Mom to show us how to do it. There must have been other things she would rather have been doing when she asked me to lay my hands flat on the counter, because she pressed the Emery stick against my cuticles until my nails turned white.

"That hurts," I said.

"No, it doesn't," she said as firmly as she continued pushing.

We were seven and eight when our parents took my sister and me to meet kind, tolerant and gray-haired Mrs. Gullickson, who lived in a comfortable house with a verdant lawn that sloped downhill under fruit trees and shrubs. She invited us into her quiet home and showed us her piano room with its dark, polished upright Steinway upon which sat a metronome. She showed us the music books we would use. While she talked quietly with our parents, I peeked into her sun-drenched living room with its south facing windows. I thought how pleasant it would be to spend time there on her couch. Our parents wrote a check, set a schedule, and home we went.

When my parents' commitment to piano lessons was established, Mom and Dad procured second-hand a tall upright piano painted chalk green with a broom. When Mom asked how I felt about piano lessons, I knew it would be grand to sit in Mrs. Gullickson's beautiful living room whether I played piano or not. But I had to ask …

"Could I take ballet lessons instead?"

"There isn't anyone in town who teaches ballet. We would have to take you all the way to Rochester," she said. Rochester is 26 miles away.

They had investigated! That realization warms me now, although at the time it felt like my dream had been dismissed as irrelevant.

When I was a senior in high school still unenthusiastically practicing piano, and the local teachers had run out of fortitude to deal with my compliant but uninspired musicality, my parents found a piano teacher for me - 26 miles away in Rochester.

Mr. Robarge, who played in the piano bar at an upscale restaurant called Michael's, kept at it with me throughout my senior year in high school. Bless his heart. He wanted to help me learn a more spontaneous, fun way of making music. He thought if I knew the melody of any song, I could apply it to any key using the chords in that key and play the song without written music. Alas, I could no more be spontaneous than I could read a Chinese character. I remember Mr. Robarge saying he knew I'd get the gist of what he was trying to teach me as soon as I got over being afraid of him.

I wasn't aware that I was afraid of Mr. Robarge. I had to give that idea some consideration. He was tall and he was smart, and I certainly did intimidate easily. But he needn't have taken my unease personally. I was wary with human beings in general, and with authority figures specifically, especially when I knew they were soon to discover the limitations of my abilities.

Dad had certainly tried to motivate both my sister and me musically. He gave each of us a Van Cliburn album for Christmas. Harvey Levan "Van" Cliburn, Jr. helped America save face when the Soviets got a satellite in the sky ahead of the Americans in the space race. A Texan, Van Cliburn went to Moscow in 1958 to compete in a classical music competition and, to everyone's astonishment, including the Soviet Union's, he won.

Dad promised that if Carlyn learned to play Chopin's Polonaise in A Flat, which was recorded on her Van Cliburn gift album, and if I learned to play Tchaikovsky's Piano Concerto No. 1, the piece with which Van Cliburn won the competition, Dad would give each of us a grand piano.

I never even considered the offer. It wasn't that I didn't love Tchaikovsky. Even today his Piano Concerto No.1 is my favorite classical piece. Well, who am I kidding? It is just about the only classical piece I recognize. The fact that I do recognize even one piece of classical music is something I owe to Dad.

Carlyn, on the other hand, rose to the challenge. She taught herself how to play Chopin's Polonaise. Hour after hour she worked at the piece, carefully reading the notes on the sheet music as she played haltingly. The melody was at first lost in the hesitation of the notes, but as Carlyn became more familiar with them, her fluidity increased. She began to play with feeling. The music begins with a dramatic procession, as if dancers are filing onto a ballroom floor. Then begins a lilting dance that made me want to twirl and chassé. When she felt confident, she asked Dad to sit down in his easy chair. She scooted onto the piano bench and began to play. Dad said not a word while she played, and not a word when she finished. In fact, he got up and left the room, stepping on her triumph as he went. In the kitchen he mixed himself a highball while Carlyn waited to hear "Good job!" from him. She never heard it, and she certainly never got a grand piano. Years later he tried to give her an upright Spinet he got second-hand from someone's estate. Carlyn refused to accept it.

"Give it to someone who won't resent it," was all she had to say.

~

Farm Life

And it's a hard, it's a hard, it's a hard, and it's a hard
It's a hard rain's a-gonna fall

From *A Hard Rain's A-Gonna Fall* by Bob Dylan

After two years in town, Mom and Dad rented a tall white clapboard farmhouse that nestled privately among even taller Silver Maple trees a few miles west of Spring Valley. Their decision to move, I believe, was motivated by the scrutiny of some of the small-town residents who made note of when Dad's patrol car was in the driveway and when it was not. The farm we moved to was managed for an absentee landlord by Lloyd Russler, whose own farm and family of four kids were a mile north up the gravel road, our closest neighbors. Lloyd was a tall, tan, lean man who was always outside working on one project or another between the two properties. I never saw the man stand still.

The two bedrooms in the farmhouse were upstairs. Our parents gave us girls the larger bedroom with a picture window overlooking the gravel driveway, while they slept in the smaller room with the peaceful view of the leafy front yard.

Carlyn and I thought our bedroom was the best room in the house! The picture window with its diamond-shaped panes and a separate double-hung window to each side of it, was an incredible vantage place from which to assess any clouds scuttling in, watch red-headed woodpeckers pound their beaks into the trunks of the Silver Maples, and to see in general who was coming and going. We could see clear across Lloyd's soybean field to the south, all the way to a fencerow populated with whip-poor-wills, American Elms and a fearsome thicket of nettles taller than we were.

One of the most fascinating features of our room was a floor grate set into the linoleum that could be opened if we wanted to spy on the occupants of the dining room below or closed to hold private counsel.

A banister around the top of the stairwell outside our bedroom served as pretend horses. My horse-crazy sister loved to climb up and straddle the railing she named Blacky. Now and then I would accompany her on my pretend banister horse, Whitey.

Just off the stairwell was a long closet built into the eaves of the house. It provided useful storage for some of our family's seldom used items. One intriguing storage container in that closet was a cardboard barrel with a metal lid. One afternoon when Mom was probably out in the garden, my sister and I pried the lid off the barrel to see what was inside. We found a beautiful long white nylon nightgown trimmed in pale pink satin that I imagine was part of Mom's trousseau. It was the most beautiful gown we had ever seen. It had a drawstring satin cord for a belt. The bodice was made from two pieces of loose white fabric that hung gracefully from pink satin cords at the shoulders. We both tried it on. Carlyn sat on the banister and imagined herself galloping a horse with the gown flowing in the breeze, while I imagined myself twirling across a dance floor. I held the skirt high so that it fluttered around me as I spun in circles. We giggled as we described our fantasies to each other. Oh, but we had forgotten that the floor grate was open.

"What are you girls doing?" Mom called up the stairs.

"Nothing," we answered in unison.

"If you're playing with my negligée, I want you to stop right now!"

We quickly stuffed the nightgown back into the barrel and shut the lid.

We went outside to explore the farm. Everything we saw was new to us. Once we had looked in every outbuilding, climbed the ladder to the barn's suffocating hay loft, and strolled through the shady pasture north of the house, we went to have a look at the livestock.

Our new home was on a working farm. Lloyd kept maybe 50 Herefords and two dozen pigs at the farm. It was fun in a scary way to sit on the top rail of the fence by the barn and watch the cattle crowd in for hay or sileage. They intimidated me when they swung their heads around as if to show off their horns. When they made eye contact and lowed at me, I would climb down from the fence and go have a look at the less intimidating pigs.

The pigs were not necessarily friendly, but they were indifferent to us and preferred to root in the dirt. Their snorting was more conversational, though once in a while, one of them would squeal a nerve-shattering protest of the rude behavior of a fellow pig. I concluded that these animals couldn't be completely trusted either.

The earthy smell of the cattle and the almost sweet smell of the pigs didn't bother me, but the powerful smell of fermenting pea vine that was fed to the cattle made my eyes cross. The only refuge from the smell was inside the house with the windows closed.

Forced back inside where we could breathe through our noses again, we girls remembered Mom's fancy nightgown in the barrel upstairs. We knew we shouldn't touch it, but we must have figured we could sneak a quick and secret look at it with no harm done. Stealthily we opened the barrel and took out the nightgown. One thing led to another and soon we each tried it on again. Carlyn rode Blacky, letting the night gown drape over the rail behind her, and I spun in circles while humming a waltz when it was my turn to wear it. While I pirouetted Carlyn must have gotten bored with our games of pretend. She left me alone and hopped nonchalantly down the stairs. When she popped out of the stairwell into the dining room below, she screamed a heart-stopping shriek that froze me mid twirl. Through the floor vent Mom had heard us playing with her nightgown, hid behind the stair door, and reached out and grabbed Carlyn as she came through the door. I could hear Mom's hand cracking against my sister's behind.

"I told you girls not to play with my negligée! Don't you ever do that again!"

Terrorized, I quickly pulled the nightgown over my head, stuffed it back in the barrel and vowed to never go downstairs again as long as I lived. Hearing Mom's feet crashing up the stairs I cowered on the floor by the register and braced myself for her blows. Mercifully she only clunked me on the head with the thimble on the tip of her finger, but the hateful look she gave me was as powerful as a blow. I knew my sister and I were guilty, but I had no idea that we had transgressed as egregiously as the punishment indicated.

There must be a story about that negligée that she guarded as fiercely as the gown itself. We never saw her wear the gown. She didn't talk about the gown. Yet she kept the gown. I will never know what it meant to her.

~

Mrs. Best

*Female friendships that work are relationships in which
women help each other to belong to themselves.*

Louise Bernikow

Most of the farm out-buildings stood empty since the center of Lloyd's industry was the farm up the road. The empty buildings on this site presented Dad with an opportunity. Trained in auto-body repair, he had always wanted to restore a vintage automobile, and now not only did he have a place to do that, but he had recently located a Ford Model A convertible in Iowa. For a couple of hot summer days our parents left us in the care of a baby-sitter who came to stay with us while they drove south to pick up the jalopy.

I'm sorry I do not remember our baby-sitter's name. I will call her Mrs. Best because she was the best babysitter ever, Mrs. Doubtfire notwithstanding. Mrs. Best was a tall, white-haired retired woman who dressed in pants instead of a house dress. Her grin was mischievous, and her short hair left her long earlobes exposed.

Mrs. Best wasn't shy about her earlobes. She explained to us how they came to be so long. When she was our age she lived on a farm, too, she told us. Sometimes when she went out for a stroll around her farm, she would sink into a manure pile. To save her, her dad had to cast a fishing line, snag an ear lobe with the hook and pull her to safety.

As soon as she told us her silly story, we fell in love with her. We offered to take her out for a safe walk around our farm, and she delighted us by agreeing to come. The shady north pasture was the perfect place to walk on a hot day, and even better, there were no cattle in that particular pasture. We squeezed through strands of fencing where gnarly oaks grew with dark green leathery leaves. A few trees had been cut down and their stumps left behind. It was Mrs. Best's idea that one of us stand on a stump and deliver a church service, this being Sunday morning.

I climbed up and faced Carlyn and Mrs. Best who seated themselves on stumps of their own. My sermon had only just begun when Mrs. Best cleared her throat and pointed out that someone in the congregation was chewing gum. Carlyn! Scandalous! Carlyn had to stand up on her stump in mock shame while I gave a giggling blessing of cats, dogs and trees. I was about to adjourn church when Mrs. Best hinted I might want to forgive the gum chewer, which I did. Then it was Carlyn's turn to give a sermon, and Mrs. Best pointed out to her that someone was giggling in church. It was my turn to stand up on my stump and listen to Carlyn's sermon. We were all giggling then, even Mrs. Best, so the sermon ended with each of us standing on a stump.

The next day Carlyn and I were playing with our dolls in the shady front yard when we heard the phone ring through the screen door. Mrs. Best took the call, and then asked us to get our dog and come inside. The phone call was from Mrs. Russler who called to warn us that a heat-crazed Hereford had crashed through their fence. The steer was running straight down the gravel road toward our house in pursuit of the Russler's hired man. The hired man was actually baiting the beast, keeping it moving toward a place it could be contained – our farm. We watched from the living room window. Soon the farm hand jogged into view with a very intense, well-muscled rusty red and white bovine trotting purposefully behind him. Flecks of foam spewed from the panting mouth of the stressed beast. Its crazed wide eyes bulged in a stare locked onto the man it intended to skewer to the ground. In contrast, the hired man looked like he was enjoying this skip down the road. He wore a familiar smile – he was a high-school kid who rode the school bus with us – that said he was not fatigued and, in fact, confident that he had this brute under control.

The three of us and our dog went from window to window watching as the boy danced along in front of the berserk whiteface drawing him around the house into our back yard. When the Hereford followed the boy into an abandoned chicken coop, we all screamed. When the wily boy popped out an open window and ran around and closed the door on the beast, we all cheered. To our great relief the monster was trapped.

Lloyd drove up in a dusty, dented pick-up truck, and the unperturbed boy sauntered over to him as if he'd simply stepped off the bus. Together they went to the window of the coop and looked in. The steer had collapsed and lay panting inside. Only minutes later we were shocked to learn it was dead. As word spread, farmers we didn't know drove into our driveway to have a look and hear the tale. There was speculation whether the animal had suffered heat stroke. As for me, I gave the coop a wide berth until Lloyd cut a hole in the side of it, attached a chain to the animal's hind legs and the other end to his tractor hitch. The tractor snorted like the steer itself as it dragged the carcass out near the barn to await the rendering company. Did we have story to tell Mom and Dad when they got home that evening, towing Dad's Model A!

Some days later Mom accompanied Carlyn and I out back by the barn to have a look at the steer's body. We stood back about 30 feet while our dog sniffed the rank animal. Still obsessed with the adventures that had occurred while our parents had been out of town, we asked Mom if she would like to see where we had played church with Mrs. Best. We were thrilled she obliged. Before we stepped through the strands of wire at the north pasture fence, Mom pointed out the top strand of thin wire attached to the fence posts by white enamel knobs.

"Would you touch that?" she asked me, grinning as she tipped her head toward the wire.

"Sure," I said, ignoring my something-is-up instinct, my why-is-she-grinning question at the back of my mind. I reached out and wrapped my hand around the wire.

A shock jangled my arm all the way to the shoulder. I yelled and jumped back.

Mom laughed uproariously.

"Didn't you know it's electric?" she laughed mirthfully.

Turning toward Carlyn Mom repeated, "She didn't know it's electric!"

I'm not sure Carlyn knew the wire was electric either, but she laughed along with equal delight.

For just a second, I puzzled whether I had done something I should be embarrassed about, but no, the way the two of them laughed I must have done something entertaining. I gave myself credit then for being a hilarious kid-version of Jerry Lewis.

And I'm sure Mom credited herself for being a fun mom, telling herself she was just as much fun as Mrs. Best.

In September when school resumed, the bus delivered us home one afternoon where I was horrified to see that the entire herd of beef cattle at our farm was loose. They wandered lazily across our driveway, checked out what was still growing in Mom's vegetable garden, munched on clover in the backyard, and in general behaved, I imagined, like the heat-crazed steer, hungry predators waiting to rip small schoolgirls into bite sized pieces. I stood on the bottom step of the open bus door watching my sister casually walk from the bus to the house. Hesitating, estimating my speed against the Herefords' distance from the bus, I knew I would have to make a dash or face abominable shame from the judgment of the other kids. Those kids picked up on my reluctance to step off the bus.

"Holy cow! You afraid of a cow?"

"Sissy city kid!"

"Cow gonna' bite you?"

I launched from the step, and despite my terror it's likely not a single animal batted an eye as I raced pall mall to the kitchen door. By suppertime Lloyd, mounted on a sorrel horse with a western saddle, rounded up all the child-munching cattle and returned them to their repaired pasture.

On another evening after supper which was served early to accommodate Dad's evening patrol shift, Carlyn, tired of cartwheels, meandered into the house where Dad dressed for work and Mom washed the supper dishes. I remained on my back in the clover outside naming the shapes of early evening clouds.

When the kitchen door burst open and my sister ran screaming from the house I sat up in alarm. Without a look in my direction Carlyn ran down the driveway toward the road. I leapt to my feet. Whatever had happened had to be bad if my fearless sister who shrugged at Herefords ran as if to save her life. I looked quickly for a hiding place. Out past the coop with the steer-sized hole in its wall stood a weathered outhouse. I scrambled for it, jumped inside and latched the door. I held my breath, not because of the ancient stink of composting human waste, but so no one outside could hear my panicky breathing and locate me. A few minutes later I heard the kitchen door slam again. This time I heard Mom's voice.

"Carlyn, come back!"

Because I was too small to look out the tiny window high up the wall, I would have to unlatch the door and stick my head out if I wanted to see what was happening. When I heard my sister's wracking sobs progressing north on the road, I mustered the courage to crack the door ever so slightly and peek out. Mom outpaced my sister. As she grabbed her, Carlyn kicked and fought.

"No! No! No!"

Carlyn's face was contorted and blotchy. I couldn't hear everything Mom said, but Carlyn's screams pierced me. Quickly I pulled back inside the outhouse and re-fastened the door. I was prepared to remain in the outhouse for the rest of my life if need be. Ordinarily I would have amused myself by paging through the remains of a yellowing Sears & Roebuck Catalog that lay on the wooden bench if I hadn't been too anxious to think about anything except what was happening outside.

After ten or 15 minutes I heard a car pull out of the driveway – Dad's patrol car? It grew quiet. I barely breathed. Another ten minutes ticked by. Mom called my name from way off by the kitchen door. I did not answer. Another five minutes later the outhouse door rattled.

"Kathy, are you in there?"

I did not answer.

"You can come out. Everything is fine."

I did not move.

"Kathy, come out now."

Although this was a command, Mom's voice did not sound threatening. I felt compelled to unlatch the door. Mom pulled the door open.

"What's wrong?" I asked before I stepped out.

"Nothing,'" she lied. "Come in the house."

She took me by the hand, I think, to ensure that I came with her rather than to comfort me.

When we stepped into the kitchen Carlyn was there. She looked haunted, edgy, but her eyes were dry.

"Where's Daddy?" she asked. Her voice was angry, not fearful.

"He left for work."

"Is he coming back?"

"I don't know."

An empty feeling settled into my stomach.

No one said much. Night came on. We were sent to bed, but we did not sleep.

"What happened?" I whispered when my sister and I were alone in the darkness.

"I heard Daddy and Mommy arguing in the bathroom. When I pushed open the door, I saw Daddy slap Mommy's face," she said as she lay on her back staring up at the darkened ceiling.

Her voice got tight and squeaky. Her eyes clenched so hard that tears squeezed out and ran down the sides of her face toward her ears.

Daddy slapped Mommy. I don't remember being particularly shocked at this information. People slap people. Except Daddy was the nice one. I had never known Daddy to slap anyone. Mommy had always said our Daddy was the greatest Daddy in the world. The three of us orbited around him. Carlyn and I competed to sit closest to Daddy in the car, at the table, in church. But Carlyn had seen him slap Mommy with her own eyes. I wondered if Mommy had done something mean to Daddy. After a while I sat up waiting to see the headlights of the patrol car turn into the driveway. I fell asleep without seeing them.

In the morning while my sister and I ate our Post Grape-nuts cereal I was surprised to hear Dad's feet coming down the squeaky wooden stairs. He stepped into the kitchen where we sat at the table with our cereal spoons halfway to our mouths. He said nothing, no words of greeting, no words of explanation, no words of apology. We had nothing to say either. We just watched him carefully. Our eyes on him must have felt weighty. Instead of sitting down and joining us for breakfast he went outside, got in the family car, and drove away without a word to anyone about where he was going, what he was going to do, or when he would be back.

He did come back later in the day, and life went on very much like normal, except that a sense of wariness came with him. It moved in to stay and became a part of – if not our entire family – me.

When the landlord, Lloyd Russler's boss, and his family moved to Spring Valley, our family was given notice. They would move into "our" farmhouse. Mom and Dad found a two-bedroom upstairs apartment on Huron Avenue in town. We moved there while our parents began looking for acreage on which to build a house of our own.

~

Odd Duck

The beatings will continue until the morale improves.

Common phrase of undetermined origin

"May I go to the bathroom?" I asked Mrs. Koebke, my second-grade teacher.

Permission granted, I stepped out of the classroom and carefully closed the door just in time to see Mr. Skagerberg raise a two-foot long heavy wooden paddle and smack it down hard on a little boy's backside. Across the wide corridor from where I stood a large window framed the view into the principal's office. Mr. Skagerberg raised the paddle and struck the child two more times with all his apparent strength. The boy's screams and the cracks of the paddle echoed through the principal's closed door and out into the open space where I watched, a lone and horrified witness.

Holding the writhing boy by one arm Mr. Skagerberg, red in the face, hollered, "What do you have to say for yourself now?"

Shrieking was all the boy had to say.

I raced to the bathroom, hoping Mr. Skagerberg hadn't seen me.

Now that we lived in town my sister and I no longer took the bus to school. We walked roughly a mile, about a 15-minute walk. Every morning we left our house early enough to get to school on time, but then we backtracked two or three lots up the street to meet up with three of the Jorgenson kids and sometimes with their neighbors, the pretty girls with the hung-over mother who yelled at her daughters from her bed while we waited in the doorway.

After seeing the punishment our principal was capable of, it killed me to have to wait for our friends' moms to dole out lunch money, or to wait for jackets to be donned. I goaded, cajoled and urged my sister and our schoolmates to hurry. To make matters worse, Carlyn and our neighbors talked as they walked instead of focusing on the primary goal: avoiding a paddling for being late. My vigorous gait was supposed to motivate them, but instead it frequently gave them something to laugh about. Since I was the only one who actually saw Mr. Skagerberg use his paddle, I was the only one who believed he most definitely would use it on us.

To allow for an earlier departure to school I started getting up at 5:00 AM to put our family's breakfast on the table. By 5:05 I was dressed for school. By 5:10 I had bacon frying in the pan, the orange juice poured, and the breakfast table set. By 5:15 I began hounding my parents and sister to get up. My sister had as much riding on a swift start as I did, but she was nearly as cranky as my parents about this early awakening.

The plan came to a head the morning I accidentally stuck a wet thumb in the electric toaster on the kitchen counter. The voltage of the toaster wasn't enough to do more than prickle, but already wound up with anxiety I let out a high-pitched scream.

Dad dashed into the kitchen wearing nothing but his briefs.

"Get back in bed right now! Don't get up until I tell you to!" he roared.

He could have let it go at that, but he added a whipping with a belt for emphasis. In all fairness, he didn't put much snap into the swing of the belt. I guess he didn't expect my fearful screams to be as penetrating as they were. Maybe he worried they would wake our landlady who lived downstairs. Nevertheless, I now was damned if I got up early, and damned if I got up late. I never walked to school with the other kids again. I lit out on a run to school by myself for the rest of the time we lived there. A person never knew who would turn on them next.

~

Dad

I stand before you as a tower of strength, the weight of the
world on my shoulders. As you pass through my life, look, but
not too close, for I fear I will expose the vulnerable me.

Deidra Sarault

In 1958 Spring Valley third graders were taught a course on Native Americans. It was a one-sided rosy overview: Euro-American pioneers moved in, and Natives moved out, as depicted - until 2023 - on Minnesota's state flag. Unapologetic to the original Minnesotans who are indigenous people, our flag depicted Natives riding toward the setting sun as white settlers plowed their land. None of the ruthless acts of white greed, theft, racism, and genocide that sent many aborigines into the twilight were mentioned. The objective of our school curriculum seemed to be to teach the history of our state with a polite nod to our first people. As irrelevant as our Natives may have been to our school board, the fact that an entire unit was devoted to them in 1958 long before Critical Race Theory was a concept in the white mind, seems remarkable, even though no native speakers were invited in to tell third graders their stories or personal experiences. There was no focus on the specific tribes who lived in Minnesota, and certainly no mention of the largest mass hanging in the United States when in 1862 38 starving Dakota were put to death in Mankato after daring to retaliate for broken treaties and theft. Nevertheless, I am profoundly grateful that our school introduced us to the subject, because up until then I was oblivious about the State's Native history – and my own.

At home I told Mom about our new unit of study.

"You know your daddy is Indian, don't you?"

"He is?" I asked, astounded.

"You don't know that?" She sounded equally astounded.

If Dad ever talked to me about his heritage, which I doubt he did, I hadn't paid attention. It certainly never occurred to me that my handsome uncles and beautiful aunts were the Chippewa or, as I later came to know them, the Anishinabeg, the name they called themselves.

Kids don't ask, "Uncle Willis, why do you have such thick, glossy black hair?"

Kids don't ask, "Aunt Doris, where did your deep brown eyes come from?"

Kids don't ask, "Dad, why do the corners of your eyes tilt down?"

Kids simply accept that that's how their relatives come.

"MY dad is part INDIAN," I bragged to my classmates, to his chagrin I now reckon.

To a grade schooler studying the hunters of buffalo, the makers of birch bark canoes, the brewers of Maple syrup, my pride couldn't have been more resplendent if I had just learned Elvis Presley was a blood relative.

I was all about Indians from that point on. It was dumbfounding to have to explain to our elderly landlady what I thought she should know already: that pemmican was the Native American version of trail mix. As I pulled little blue berries off her shrubs for my own experimental pemmican recipe, it never occurred to me that she asked what I was doing not because she cared, but because she wanted me to leave her junipers alone.

I'm guessing the year was 1959, the end of a decade, when my family drove up to Bloomington from Spring Valley to visit Dad's brother Earl and his wife on New Year's Eve. Uncle Earl, who drove a caterpillar for building contractor Marvin Anderson, had been invited with his family to a New Year's Eve party at his boss' house.

That New Year's Eve, Uncle Earl's "family" included not just his wife, but my parents, my sister and me for lack of a babysitter, and one adult cousin, Marvin, from the Milwaukee area who was attending college in Mankato and did not want to be alone on the holiday. We all arrived at a new rambler in a treeless subdivision under a starless black sky in sub-zero cold. The adults in an eager party state of mind laughed and joked in clouds of breath as they jogged to the door. We descended to the basement of the home where there was a built-in bar. Card tables and folding chairs were set up across the concrete floor. Cigarette smoke and boring grown-up talk quickly stupefied my sister and me. We were put to bed in the hostess' bedroom with the promise that our cousin would awaken us at midnight to see in the New Year. Despite the hilarity coming from the basement, we fell asleep under a pile of guests' coats. When Mom woke us in the wee hours of New Year's morning, there was no celebration underway. Carlyn and I were disappointed we had slept through it. We were ushered out of the too quiet house to the frosty car without being asked to say a proper thank you to the hostess. Nor was our hostess at the door saying a proper goodbye. The frozen bench-style back seat of the car did not yield when we sat down on it. In contrast to our arrival, no one spoke.

Back at Uncle Earl's we were put to bed again and slept until late in the morning. I don't know if it was the snoring itself that woke us or the rattling of all the house windows each time an inhuman wheeze issued from our aunt and uncle's bedroom. As the adults awoke, one by one they shuffled bleary eyed to the kitchen in search of coffee.

Sitting unobtrusively in the next room my sister and I overheard what we had slept through the night before.

"How many stitches did they give him?" someone asked.

Someone else answered, "Twenty! Didn't you see his eyebrow was sewn from end to end?"

Apparently sometime after midnight Dad stood up to sing the Lord's Prayer to the revelers. Why the Lord's Prayer instead of Auld Lange Syne was never explained. Although Dad was no Mario Lanza, he could sing. One of the merrymakers took offense, however. Maybe the person requested Auld Lange Syne; maybe Dad didn't know the words, so instead sang a song he knew.

At any rate, the affronted individual said something like, "Who does that drunken Indian think he is?"

That's when Uncle Earl swung his fist. The fellow swung back. Each adult had their own details to add to what Uncle Earl later described as a "donnybrook". I pictured a scene like something out of a John Wayne movie: the cowboys versus three Indians, Dad, Uncle Earl and our cousin

Marvin. But it was someone more formidable than the sheriff who put a stop to the fight. It was the outraged hostess who would not abide a blood-staining brawl in her new home.

That was the first time I had inklings that racial prejudice exists in Minnesota; that there might be good reason why Dad didn't speak of his heritage; and that drinking copious amounts of alcohol and exercising good judgment never occupied the same time and place.

Once almost three decades later Dad and I drove together to visit Dad's cousin Opal who lived on the White Earth Reservation, the place of Dad's birth, in northwest Minnesota. I hadn't been there since I was an unaware kid, so it never struck me until this visit that white families lived here. Many white families. White families mowing their lawns, washing their cars, water skiing.

"What are all these white people doing here?" I asked Dad, puzzled. "I thought this was an Indian reservation."

As he steered the car along the scenic curves of the highway his eyebrows furrowed as if he was working out an answer, but he did not speak. The reservation we drove through in the late 1980s was a shocking patchwork of less than 10% of its original 800,000 acres.

I found answers for both of us when I picked up a book by Melissa L. Meyer with a provocative title, *The White Earth Tragedy*[6] (Meyer). Five years after the Dakota uprising and subsequent execution of the 38, the government came up with a unilateral solution to "the Indian problem" in Minnesota. They set aside the aforementioned 800,000 acres of land and promised all the Minnesota Chippewa who agreed to move there up to 160 acres of their own to farm. Any excess land that remained was to be opened for sale to anyone.

The government believed the Indians would be grateful to learn the respectable lifestyle of European farming. Either the government hadn't listened very well to the Natives, or they hadn't trusted that "inherently backward" people could be self-determining.

Of course, the Natives knew the land was valuable. It had been their home for eons, but they used the land differently. Instead of cutting down every tree to sell for lumber or plowing every inch of land to grow crops for sale, they used the land communally. They weren't capitalists, and they didn't consider themselves to be poor. They migrated seasonally, tapping Maple trees in spring, hunting buffalo and elk along the Red River in summer, ricing in lake shallows in late summer and fishing in winter. They shared with each other what they harvested, and that lifestyle had worked for them for centuries.

The White Earth Treaty required "full-bloods" to keep their land for 25 years to allow time for assimilation to Euro-American culture. "Mixed bloods", who some government officials believed were more competent, were permitted to sell their land. And of course, it was the government who made the legal determination of whether a person was a "full" or "mixed blood". Was it a coincidence that, "officially", the majority of Natives enrolled at White Earth happened to be "mixed bloods"? While the state and federal governments were busy assessing (via unscientific methods such as scratching Native's skin to see the color of their blood) racial quantum, there were white buyers chomping at the border of the reservation. They were ready to offer the "mixed bloods" a "deal" for their land.

It was a boon to many of them that some of the Anishinabeg did not know how to handle American money. Cagey settlers would sometimes dupe an Indian for their acreage, without much apparent guilt. It must have seemed a travesty to them that those Indians didn't know how to put the land to "proper" use.

To the Natives, "full blooded" only connoted the practice of traditional ways no matter what percentage of Indian blood was in their lineage. And, of course, every race has their share of hoodwinkers. Some "full bloods" who wanted to sell claimed to be "mixed bloods". If the "chipmunks" were silly enough to believe the "full bloods" and give money to one person for land that belonged to all of them, that Native would take the money and laugh at the gullibility. By the time the Natives realized land titles were no joke, they were homeless.

Allotment of land, the chance to own 160 acres for a song, is what brought Dad's Welsh grandfather, John Erion, and his wife, Almira Hunt, to White Earth. How they acquired their land I don't want to know.

What I do know is that all John's children said their father, my great grandfather, was a drunk. Whether the cause of this disease alcoholism is nature or nurture, none of John's children ever took the risk to drink liquor. They had witnessed first-hand what liquor in the wrong hands can do to a family.

One of John's teetotaling sons, my Grandpa Oliver, fell in love with a native girl. Her Anishinabe name was Mayshkowegahbowequay. Anishinabe language students tell me this may mean "foreigner" or "traveler". Why would my great grandparents name their little girl "Foreigner"? Anishinabeg sometimes give a person a new name in recognition of a significant event in their lives. Leaving family for a few hours on the first day of kindergarten is significant enough. Imagine at the age of five being taken away from your family to live in a boarding school where a different language is spoken, where an alien religion is taught, where unfamiliar clothing is worn, where no one kisses you goodnight.

The teachers didn't use Mayshkowegahbowequay's native name. They gave her a name they could pronounce: Sarah. The foreignization of Mayshkowegabowequay was underway. Here I have to ask whether my Grandma Erion felt like a foreigner, a stranger, an alien, an oddity, in the company of the white people living in her community.

Because Oliver grew up on reservation land, he didn't take Sarah for a foreigner. She looked like many other young people on the Res. What he took her for was smart, funny and sweet. Oliver and Sarah were 20 and 18 respectively when they married, and they had a baby on the way. We grandchildren are left to read between the lines to speculate how the news of Grandpa's marriage to an "Indian" was received by his family. One of Oliver's cousins simply recorded in their journal that "Oliver married an Indian[!]" The exclamation mark is mine, because nothing else was noted about her. Oliver's brothers' white wives' full names and ages were listed in that journal.

Dad was born to Oliver and "Sarah" on February 14, 1918, six years before Native Americans had the right to vote. Grandma named Dad Valentine. I'm sure she believed there could be no more perfect a name for her darling baby. Dad always claimed he never forgave his mother's choice of his name. Whatever he thought, his daughters loved Grandma's name choice. Dad was our personification of a Valentine like he had been Grandma's, and we always celebrated his birthday with delight.

Mayshkowegahbowequay and Oliver had six children before Grandma died of an ulcerated gallbladder just short of her 36th birthday. The youngest, Aunt Iris, was only one year old when Grandma died; Uncle Earl was five; Aunt Doris was ten; Dad was 12; Uncle Willis was 14; Aunt Ruby was 16. Grandpa scrambled to find care for his children while he worked to support them. Ruby got married. Willis went to work. Grandpa's brother Frank and his schoolteacher wife Emma volunteered to take Dad so he could stay in school through eighth grade. Aunt Doris went to the Catholic boarding school in White Earth where her mother had been educated. The two littlest kids went to live with Oliver's parents, John (the drunk) and Almira Erion.

Aunt Doris became sick at the Sisters' School – sick enough that the school sent for Oliver and asked him to take her home. "Home" at that time was John and Almira's. Doris recovered under Almira's care, but there was a new challenge: Grandpa John.

Rebuffed by Doris when he tried to grab her and lift her skirt, John's retort to his granddaughter was, "You're nothing but a dirty little Indian!" Again, we grandchildren can only speculate that if a sweet innocent child was referred to as a "dirty little Indian" by her own grandfather, that her siblings must have been regarded similarly. And, of course, there would have been repercussions.

Dad eventually enrolled in the Flandreau Indian Boarding School in South Dakota where he lettered in music and earned his high school diploma. When he graduated, he went on to learn auto-body repair. That was his vocation when World War II began. He was drafted into the United States Army in 1941. Because of Dad's excellent long-distance vision, he was enrolled in pilot training. When the European Allies decided to launch the infamous Battle of the Bulge, every available soldier who could be spared was reassigned, thus ending his flight training.

For his service during the Battle of the Bulge, Dad was awarded a

Bronze Star. Typically, Dad never talked about the event that earned him that honor.

In later years Aunt Doris told me she believed the Bronze Star was awarded because Dad awakened and rescued his squad when the barn they were sleeping in was about to be bombed by German aircraft. She went on to say that what Dad suffered in the war made him an alcoholic. Though the suffering was considerable, experience has since taught me that hardship and suffering don't "make" anyone an alcoholic, or wouldn't everyone be an alcoholic?

~

Life at Alma's

Dreams like you are making now
Are very hard to share
All I ask is one small favor
Dream a dream and wish me there

From *Blue on Blue* by Joni Mitchell

As kids my sister and I used to keep the empty six-ounce frozen orange juice concentrate cans our breakfast juice came from. We thought it was fun to drink out of them because they were child sized and had colorful pictures of oranges on them. These versatile tin cans could be handy for picnics in the backyard, or even for washing paint brushes. One gray and chilly day as I prepared to paint a watercolor masterpiece, I filled an orange juice can with 7-Up for myself while I laid out my tray of paints on a card table. I carried another can to the garage and filled it with turpentine which Dad used when he cleaned his brushes after painting the pasture fence. I did not know watercolor paint brushes could be cleaned in water. If Dad cleaned paint brushes with turpentine, that was the proper way.

I was well into my painting when Dad announced that lunch was ready. It was just the two of us that day. Mom and Carlyn were off running errands. I set my paintbrush in one can and took the last gulp of 7-Up from the other before heading to the kitchen. My hair stood on end when I realized I had a mouthful of pine-sap turpentine. I spit the turpentine back into the can as my eyes watered.

Did any go down my throat?

Will this kill me?

If I tell Daddy I did this, will he kill me?

With trepidation I walked to the kitchen, waiting for pangs of death to seize me.

How much will it hurt? I wondered.

Dad set sandwiches on the table for us. Braunschweiger, Swiss cheese, mustard, and mayo on white bread with a ring of onion, a slice of tomato lightly salted, and a fringe of lettuce – one of Dad's favorite lunches. Dad seated himself at the head of the kitchen table. Neither one of us spoke. Expecting nausea, a cramp, a constriction of my throat I sat down tentatively along the side of the table. Dad was half-way through with his sandwich when he noticed I hadn't eaten anything.

"You had better eat."

I picked up the sandwich, took a tentative bite and swallowed. I waited. Nothing. I took another bite of the sandwich and waited. Still nothing.

"Daddy…" I started.

My voice drew his eyes to me from some distant, grown-up place.

"If someone drank turpentine, what would happen to them?"

He shrugged. "It would probably depend on how much they drank."

I waited for him to say more. He did not. His eyes returned to staring at that invisible thing that needed his concentration while he munched his sandwich.

Considering his answer, and the lack of any pain, I went ahead and ate my sandwich. When we finished, we silently put our plates in the sink. Dad washed and set them in the dish rack to dry while I went back to my watercolor.

The diluted blues were cold. The lavender was weak like the gray sky outside. These bleak colors left me with a hollow feeling – something akin to being alone in the world. I was certain if I died from turpentine, my family would be mad that I had wasted good turpentine. I scrunched up the paper, emptied my cans and went outside to talk to the dog.

~

Tennis Shoes

So take a good look at my face
You'll see my smile looks out of place
If you look closer, it's easy to trace
The tracks of my tears

From *The Tracks of My Tears* by Smokey Robinson,
Pete Moore and Marv Tarplin

I stood at the bathroom sink washing a pair of white tennis shoes by hand because they couldn't be laundered in the wringer washing machine that Mom still used. Gray marks on these shoes were scars of frustrated efforts to avoid toe stubs and puddles. Mom sat in the bathtub directing my effort while she bathed.

"No! Not like that. Under the water."

I pushed my hands into the warm soapy water. A shoe bobbed up. I grabbed it too quickly. Water sloshed over the edge of the basin.

"Oh, for Pete's sake! What is wrong with you?"

In the mirror above the sink I could see the reflection of her face as red as her pendulous nipples that dipped in the steaming bath water. Careful to avoid another splash, I put a hand inside each shoe and rubbed the canvas tops against each other.

"Under the water!"

I submerged my hands still inside the shoes. Bubbles broke the surface.

"Now scrub them against each other."

I did as told, and water sloshed. Mom groaned crossly.

"Wipe that up!"

I reached for a towel hanging nearby. Water dripped from my hands. As I stooped to wipe up the drips on the linoleum, splatters fell from my eyes.

"For crying out loud!"

Yes. No use crying silently. She sees all, so cry out loud. My face tightened into a knot of pained frustration.

"Oh, stop it! I'll take care of it myself," she commanded as she levered herself to her feet with her hands on the edges of the porcelain tub.

Steam rose off her body, and bath water slid off her like a waterfall thundering into the sea.

I fled the bathroom, crossed the kitchen in two strides and was down the outside staircase before Mom's feet touched the bathmat.

~

Argument

Oh the jealousy, the greed is the unraveling
It's the unraveling
And it undoes all the joy that could be

From *All I Want* by Joni Mitchell

Not long after that when my sister and I were already in bed for the night, we lay in the dark listening to Mom and Dad's escalating dispute in the bedroom next to ours. There was an issue at stake that was more important than whoever might overhear their argument.

None of their words made sense to me.

Some of the words Mom shouted with emphasis: "She…" and "Her…".

She who? I wondered. Was the "she" the something or someone Dad thought about when he stared into space over his Braunschweiger sandwich?

Or was Mom talking about me? What had I done wrong now? I pulled my pillow over my head, but it didn't muffle their voices. It didn't sound like either one of my parents was going to back down this time.

"I don't have to listen to this!" Dad's voice.

"Then get out. I don't want you here!" Mom's voice.

"Fine!" Feet pounded on the floor. The closet door rattled. Drawers were jerked open, then slammed closed. I heard what must have been a suitcase bang against a doorjamb.

My stomach was tight as I listened to Dad march through the living room toward the front door. I expected Mom to try to stop him, but she didn't. She didn't leave their bedroom. She didn't call him back. I sat up in bed in disbelief, but I would not insert myself in their quarrel. Not so my sister. She leapt out of bed and ran to the living room.

"Don't go, Daddy! Don't go!" she screamed.

"Your Mommy doesn't want me here anymore," he said in a pitiful voice.

I understood if Mommy was nicer, Daddy would stay.

"I want you here!" answered Carlyn with heartbreak in her voice.

I heard the squeak of the rocking chair springs. One of them must have sat down. Carlyn stayed out there with him, sobbing in the dark. After a long time, she climbed back in bed, still crying. When we awoke in the morning I stayed where I was. I would stay in bed for the rest of my life or at least until someone gave me a signal that it was safe to get up. But my sister jumped up and ran out to see if Dad was still there.

"You're here!"

This time I heard relief in her voice. Neither parent said a word to us about what happened the night before, and I wasn't about to ask.

Decades later I met a friendly woman about my age at a Christmas party in Edina, Minnesota. She was from Harmony or Fountain or Preston, one of the small towns of southeastern Minnesota. We bonded as soon as we learned we were both from Fillmore County. Her Dad had been a farmer. She asked what my dad did.

"He was a Highway Patrolman."

Her eyes grew large with interest.

"What did you say your last name is?"

"Erion."

"Are you any relation to Val Erion?"

"He's my father."

"Oooh," she squealed. Both her arms went up like exclamation points.

"I knew him! After my dad died, he was always so kind to my mom. He'd come out in his squad car after every snow fall. If our driveway hadn't been plowed, he'd call the county and ask them to plow it out for Mom. She just adored him!"

Unbidden, the memory of Mom shouting the words "She" and "Her" crawled down my spine. You don't suppose …?

Frankenstein

> "Tucker strokes my hair. There's something so tender about the gesture. It might as well have been him whispering I love you."

From *Hallowed* by Cynthia Hand

Spring Valley had a movie theatre on its main street in the 1950s and 60s. It's where, during a Saturday matinee, I first saw "The Wizard of Oz". It's also where when I was about 10 years old my sister and I saw *The Curse of Frankenstein*", or to be accurate, it's where my sister saw the movie.

"Can we go to the show with Cindy?" Carlyn begged Mom, careful not to name the movie.

She ever so cleverly included her friend Cindy's name to add heft to the idea that this was a child-suitable movie. It was Carlyn's greatest desire to see the "in" movie, and I went where she went. I couldn't abide being left out. If my sister rode her pony across the railroad trestle, I rode my pony across the railroad trestle, too, even if I screamed all the way across in terror of meeting a train.

I do remember Mom asking what the movie was, although there were no movie ratings then. She was wary because I had somewhat of an adverse reaction (read: movie stopping hysteria) to the giant spider in the movie *Tarantula* that the babysitter took us to when we were five and six. Either Carlyn was vague enough about the name of this new show or Mom, after some consideration, thought it would be advantageous to have both kids out of the apartment for a couple of hours while she and Dad had friends over for drinks. Triumphant, Carlyn and I raced the entire five or six blocks to the theater with no apprehension of the evening darkness.

At the theater it looked like every child in town had turned out. A throng of animated kids chattered and laughed under the lit marquis. The smell of hot buttered popcorn wafted through the double doors as we waited in line outside at the ticket window. We could hear the muffled explosions of kernels as the popcorn overflowed the popper and fell into the bottom of the machine. Inside a crush of kids at the concession counter picked out Milk Duds, Junior Mints, Life Savers and Slo-Poke suckers. We passed by the concessions - we only had money for the movie.

We found two velveteen upholstered seats next to each other in the center of the middle section. As we took our seats we waved and greeted school mates. I loved being part of the ebullient camaraderie of the audience - until the movie started. The lights dimmed. Then came a black and white news reel which we ignored as we scanned through the shadows looking for familiar faces. The news reel faded, and the screen lit up with the title of the film. Ominous music with strings and drums began, as if to warn us. Coming here might have been a bad idea.

I watched until the first glimpse of the bandaged monster. At that point, even my sister covered her eyes with her hands. When I jumped up to dash to the lobby, Carlyn was right at my heels. In the now dimly lit entry the concessions were closed, and the clerks were gone. Just the two of us stood listening to the oppressive chords of music coming from the auditorium. I begged Carlyn to go home with me. She was reluctant. As the strains of alarming music began to fade, she gravitated toward the auditorium doors.

"No, I have to see what's happening."

Her decision made, she turned and walked back into the darkness.

Alone, I paced the floor. Our family did not have a television set. Maybe that lent itself to my difficulty in differentiating reality and make-believe. If the story was possible on a movie screen, wouldn't it also be possible in real life? Looking out at the street I envisioned the monster crashing through the glass doors from the now deserted sidewalk. I considered going back into the dark auditorium, but what if Frankenstein stepped through the movie screen? At that thought I burst through those exterior doors in a panic and ran for my life toward home.

After turning off main street I flew down the meagerly lit residential streets. Every tree trunk was a potential hiding place for a swaddled monster. I kept an eye on the shadows as I sprinted past them. I gasped for air. I sobbed. Closing in on Huron Avenue I could see the blessed lights were on in our upstairs apartment. I scrambled up the outside steps two at a time. When I reached our door and was about to yank it open, the thought occurred to me that Frankenstein could be anywhere. Maybe Frankenstein waited on the other side of the door. I became hysterical - too afraid to go in and too afraid to run back down the steps. I stood on the landing bawling uncontrollably, unable to decide. Then the door opened, and Mom stood there. Or was it Mom? The woman looked like Mom, but could I be sure? I hesitated.

"What are you doing out here? Where's your sister?"

I was incapable of a coherent answer. I could barely breathe.

One of my parents' guests, a woman I did not know, stood in the entry just behind Mom. Her sympathetic voice was guidance for Mom and solace for me.

"The poor little thing is terrified!"

Mom pulled me into the foyer. I continued to cry because I could not trust that Mom would not metamorphose into the monster.

I glanced into the living room where Dad and a male guest sat talking together in normal conversational tones. The hysterics of a little girl were too inconsequential to disturb their conversation.

"Let's put you to bed," Mom said.

"Noooh!"

The last thing I wanted was to be alone in the bedroom with the lights out.

The angelic woman said to Mom, "Why don't you take her in to bed and sit with her? I'll heat up some milk for her."

Mom, who had never served anyone warm milk, looked surprised at the offer, but agreed it was a good idea.

"Angelica" warmed milk in a pan on the stove while Mom had me change into my pajamas. She sat beside me on the bed in the well-lit room while I drank the milk Angelica brought in a coffee cup. I don't remember ever having such comforting and calming attention before.

Having survived the monster, Carlyn arrived home about an hour later, no worse for having seen the entire movie than when she left the house.

The next day Mom forbid me to ever see another monster movie. That rule got no argument from me, but Carlyn made it clear she wasn't going to miss scary movies on my account. She and the neighbor kids thought I was a real sissy, but no amount of ridicule would get me to ever see another horror show.

~

Additional Peculiarities

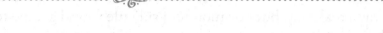

All I can do is be me, whoever that is.

Bob Dylan

Besides being an overly sensitive child, I had additional peculiarities. When I was about 12 our family went to Pimushe Resort near Black Duck, Minnesota for a week's vacation. We joined Mom's brother Forrest and his family from Kansas at the resort where they vacationed every June.

When the resort owner's jeep popped to life in the evenings signaling garbage collection time, children came running from all over the resort as if the Pied Piper of Hameln had picked up his flute. We piled happily into the open jeep, thrilled to be part of the big adventure, carrying the garbage to the dump. The stink of rotting fish guts at the dump and the buzzing of flies notwithstanding, we kids were on eager alert, hoping to see bears or racoons rooting through the foul debris for their favorite fare. Besides the excitement of seeing wildlife, I felt the wonderful sense of companionship in the company of the other kids.

One day a couple of new kids climbed aboard the jeep. They were from South Carolina. They pronounced words differently than we did, and their manner of speaking got them lots of attention. Immediately my own speech changed as if a spell had been cast on me. I strung out the long "i" sound in the word Carolina and shortened the "a" as if I had talked that way my entire life. My sister and our cousin took my new manner of speaking in stride and let me be what I considered fascinating.

By the end of the second day of dump rides and tether ball with these Carolina kids, though, one suddenly stopped in the middle of our conversation, tilted her head, furrowed her brow, looked me in the eyes and asked, "Whah do y'all talk like thaat?"

Ashamed at the confrontation but having no idea what the answer to her question was, knowing only that the jig was up, I continued the pretense while I began to sidle away.

"Laik whaat?" I asked in my best rendition of Scarlett O'Hara as I backed off from the group of kids. I left them standing as I affected a nonchalant saunter toward our cabin.

There I hid until the next day when my sister announced the South Carolina family had checked out and left the resort. In relief, I resumed playing with the rest of the kids and speaking in my native Minnesota speech pattern.

You would think I had learned my lesson, but I was not a quick study. In February of 1964 when the Beatles famously appeared on the Ed Sullivan Show for the first time, everyone, it seemed, was smitten. I wanted to be as remarkable in my small world as a British Rock Star would be.

That summer the Erions had a family reunion at the apple orchard where Aunt Doris lived in Waukesha, Wisconsin. I was 14 when my sister and I arrived at Aunt Doris' a week early to help prepare for the reunion. It was our job to sweep out the vacant barn for a dance. We may not have been effective cleaners, but we had a lot of fun getting to know our cousins from Wisconsin and Michigan whom we seldom saw.

One of the guests was a girl about my age. I don't remember her name or how we were related, but she was friendly, and I liked hanging out with her. One way to clinch a friendship, I thought, was to convince a person that I was somebody impressive. I spoke to her using an English accent.

But that night as my new friend and I stretched out in our sleeping bags side by side in the dark barn loft, the girl tentatively said, "Can I ask you something?"

"Anything," I answered in my best Paul McCartney.

"Why do you talk like that?"

It was inconceivable for me to reveal I was play-acting, and that the intriguing British girl was really an uninteresting nobody. Once again, I didn't understand how to answer the question. I had to invent a specialness, even if it was a deception. With my deception exposed my face ignited in such hot shame it must have lit up the barn. I rolled over with my back to my new friend and never spoke to her again. She tried to initiate conversations a couple more times before the reunion was over, but I did my anguished best to pretend she never existed.

~

Piano Recital

When we begin to take our failures non-seriously, it means we are ceasing to be afraid of them. It is of immense importance to learn to laugh at ourselves.

Katherine Mansfield

Every spring Mrs. Gullickson's piano students performed a recital for their parents. At the end of our concert, Mrs. Gullickson provided a generous lunch for all her students and their parents in the sunroom of her home where cozy window light beamed upon us.

Customarily both Mom and Dad attended the recitals dressed in their church clothes which in those days were dresses and hose for the women and suits and ties for the men. I wonder if Dad felt uncomfortable in Mrs. Gullickson's home, because instead of sitting with the other parents, Dad paced. I was in the music room doing my eight-year-old best to impress other kids with some inane chatter when Dad stepped into the room from the hall door. He didn't pause as he entered, but walked purposefully straight toward me without a word, grasped me by the shoulder with one hand and squeezed until pain and embarrassment silenced me. Still without saying anything, Dad continued on through the room and exited through a second door into the vacant living room. I sat where I was for a moment absorbing the uncomfortable expressions of the other kids before I, too, exited the room. In mortification I sat down on Mrs. Gullickson's couch in the room I had previously imagined relaxing in, while I listened to the cheerful voices of families in the sunroom. I sat there alone berating myself for being unrefined and improper, wishing to escape, wishing to be gone.

Five years later at another of Mrs. Gullickson's annual recitals only Mom represented us in Mrs. Gullickson's living room. Dad had run some errands early in the day and had not returned home to join us before we left for our performances. There were no cell phones in 1958 - no way to reach Dad. It's just as well. My sister and I would have brought shame down upon him again - and then on us in requital. While my sister played a beautiful accompaniment by heart, I stood beside the piano and sang the words to *Moon River* using sheet music. Our piano pieces were always played from memory. Because my singing was a last-minute addition to the program, I was granted permission to use sheet music in case of a lapse. Somewhere "round the bend" my dependable sister forgot the notes and the music stopped. She stared at me with narrowed eyes that stated the obvious: "Show me the music."

I considered what she was asking. To show her the music would be a breach of the rules as I understood them. Which was the more intolerable transgression? Letting my sister peek at the music or stopping the entire performance? Never mind that the entire performance was already stopped. Before I had more time to spend contemplating this dilemma, Carlyn snatched the sheet music from my hands, slammed it on the piano easel and resumed playing. There were startled looks on some of the parents' faces but the only shocked guffaw from the audience came out of my mother.

On the way home after Mrs. Gullickson's recital lunch we spotted Dad in the parking lot at the Highway Café astride one of our horses. He was chatting with someone who had just come out of the restaurant. Mom pulled into the lot off the highway without slowing down. Dust billowed from the gravel like a storm wind was blowing. Mom pulled the car alongside the agitated horse and the wide-eyed rider and rolled down her window.

"Where were you?" she demanded of Dad in that tone that says how good it feels to be righteous.

Dad looked caught off guard.

"You missed the recital," she announced.

"Oh! That was today?"

From the back seat of the Pontiac where Carlyn and I sat watching, we could see Dad's cheeks had turned the color of a hen-pecked rooster's comb. He truly must have forgotten because our piano lessons were Dad's dream, Dad's wish, Dad's decision. He had never missed a recital before.

With a squeal of the tires, we were back on the highway leaving Dad, dancing horse and onlooker in another burst of choking dust.

Dad rode straight home and entered the house like the lawman he was coming to even the score. The argument was just getting started.

"Don't you ever speak to me in front of anyone like you just did ever again!"

"Don't you ever miss another recital!"

"I have never missed a recital in all these years! I got the days mixed up!"

I don't remember how long they kept at it, but in the end they both caught a break. Mrs. Gullickson retired from teaching that year, and our new piano teacher didn't hold recitals.

∾

The House that Dad Built

Our house is a very, very, very fine house with two cats in the yard
Life used to be so hard
Now everything is easy 'cause of you

From *Our House* by Graham Nash

In 1958 Mom and Dad bought three acres of land on the west side of highway 63 just northwest of Spring Valley. The angle of the highway shaped our lot into a triangle. The south side was bordered by an acre of woods and the west side was bordered by cropland. Our lot itself had probably been cropland. It was flat and treeless. Nevertheless, meadowlarks loved it. They sang from the fencerows outperforming pheasants' rusty voices.

Dad built our modest two-bedroom, one-bathroom house himself, in the days before prefab homes. He laid each basement block, erected each wall stud, lifted every rafter and nailed each roof shingle. Dad built with great precision. Everything was measured twice and then again with not one thirty-second of an inch variance.

He commissioned a highway patrol buddy of his to build the natural oak kitchen cupboards. The floors throughout the house were hardwood, except for the bathroom and the kitchen. Mom picked out red and black squares of floor tile for the kitchen and red laminate countertops.

Then she went to work on a room-sized braided rug for our Early American styled living room. She had collected woolen rags for years for this project. After Mom cut the rags into strips, she pieced them into long tubes, turned them, sewed the fabric tubes end to end, and sitting on the bare floor she braided them. Once braided she coiled the lengths in an oval and, using heavy upholstery thread, stitched them together. That rug was so thick and well-made that it held up for twenty years.

When the rug was finished, Mom and Dad went with each other to pick out a brand new Early American style maple table and chairs for the dining area, and maple end tables for the living room. Then, in a luxurious extravagance, Mom ordered custom-made gold brocade drapes for the large picture window in the living room. This was a first as far as I can remember. Mom had always hand-sewn our previous curtains, drapes, bedspreads and pillows.

Dad built a bookcase into the upper half of one living room wall. This was the wall where our brand-new maple-finished piano would stand.

The first spring in our new home Mom and Dad planted a hedge of fragrant red honeysuckle shrubs as a wind buffer on the west side of the property. On the point of land at the north end of the property they put in a dozen spruce trees. Along the highway to buffer the traffic sounds they added quick-growing Lombardy poplar saplings. Together in contented cooperation my parents grew a vegetable garden. Dad rototilled the soil and picked out the seed potatoes. Mom sowed beans and peas and sweetcorn. When the peas were ripe, she made a satisfying side dish of creamed peas and new potatoes. To everyone's delight our mutt would stroll through the rows of peas and pull peapods from their bushes. He chewed the pods and all, relishing the sweet flavor just as much as the rest of us.

Dad was the Radish King. He could hardly wait three weeks for those little seedlings to develop their cherry red orbs. As soon as he discovered their hot roots had expanded, he rinsed a handful under the hose, rushed into the kitchen, dipped one radish at a time into a tiny crystal dish made just for salt, and popped the entire radish into his mouth. He chomped with satisfaction savoring one of the tastes of a summer garden.

Along the north wall of the detached two-car garage, also built by Dad, Mom put in multi-colored tuberous begonias. Closer to the highway she grew a perennial garden and later added chrysanthemums along the driveway.

Dad remodeled a used shed he had hauled in for a pony barn. Once the stalls were built, he proceeded to put up a board fence around the entire pasture. Carlyn and I willingly painted it white to give our place the allure of a Kentucky horse farm.

My parents must have been excited and proud to have created this sweet little home together, but how much Dad allowed himself to feel pride in his accomplishment I can't tell you. What I can tell you is shortly after our house was built our family drove to Bloomington to visit Uncle Earl. The Marvin Anderson company had just finished another great American subdivision, and we were excited to see the latest model homes that had opened there. Everybody, that is, except Dad. He stood outside the car parked at the curb and smoked while the rest of us went inside to have a look at the models.

I had never seen a sunken living room before and I marveled. But when I spoke those words "sunken living room" in awe within earshot of Dad, his eyes squinted, his mouth grimaced, and he bent slightly forward like a man with a bad stomachache.

It still troubles me that Dad couldn't acknowledge the interesting design of another man's building while maintaining pride in his own accomplishment. He and Mom had built a simple but quality home within their budget on three bucolic acres. It was an endeavor that deserved to be celebrated, but sadly, it looked like Dad criticized himself for not having built something grander. And don't we all?

Dinner

Where did we ever get the crazy idea that to make children do better, first we have to make them feel worse? Think of the last time you felt humiliated or treated unfairly. Did you feel like cooperating or doing better?

Jane Nelsen

After school one afternoon in the mid-1960s before Mom got home from work, I sat down on a tall wooden stool at the kitchen counter, changing gears from willing high school student to surly family member. Dad strolled in from outside, already out of his uniform and dressed in his casual pants and shirt.

"What's for supper?" he asked.

A simple question that raised my hackles. Since Mom had started working, supper was a contentious subject. Mom had been a housewife most of my life. She had always done the cooking and meal planning. Indeed, she referred to the kitchen as "my kitchen". Now that Dad had asked her to contribute to the family income, she was willing to suffer the intrusion into "her" kitchen in exchange for a meal on the table at the end of her workday. Yet somehow, the responsibility most often continued to fall on her to prepare a meal as she arrived home hungry, tired and resentful.

We had never been a family who worked things out together; who mutually created a weekly menu plan, for example. We all wanted the others to know how dissatisfied we were, but none of us was a willing listener. Perhaps no one really wanted a solution. Perhaps the argument was the objective.

When Dad insinuated that supper was my responsibility, I took the customary Erion attitude: a defensive retort. Sometimes I flung my parents' own words back at them, and this time they must have hit like bullets.

"Don't mistake me for the cook."

In a split-second Dad yanked me off the stool which clattered over onto the red and black floor. Dad backed me into the corner between the stove and the sink. He slapped both sides of my face using his hands alternately in a staccato technique he must have learned … where? Do they teach such a thing at the Highway Patrol Academy? In shock I peed on myself. When he finished slapping, he grabbed my upper arm and pulled me toward the door.

"We're going grocery shopping."

I struggled to pull away, horrified.

"No! I'm not going!"

Tightening his hold, he marched me out of the house with his fingers clenched white in a vice-like grip. He ripped open the car door and jammed me inside. I tried again.

"I can't go like this!"

Dad ignored me. Once in the driver's seat he turned the key in the ignition and tromped on the gas lest I jump out. The car barreled out of our driveway, gravel shooting out from under the tires. I sat in mortified silence for the ten minutes it took to drive into town.

Dad parked in the front row right in front of the Red Owl's big bank of windows. He flung open his door and started to get out.

"Let's go."

"I'm not going in there!" I said, shrinking down in the passenger seat.

Dad leaned over close to my face and snarled, "Yes, you are."

I did not move. He lifted his hand as if to strike. Wet pants and red cheeks notwithstanding, I unlatched the door and got out. I prayed there would be no one in the store I knew.

I followed Dad in looking neither to the right nor to the left; looking only at his shoes as they stomped all the way to the back of the store to the meat department. I did not look at the grocery choices. I have no recollection of what meat Dad selected. All I cared about was that no one see me.

The adult male clerk I had chatted with on earlier occasions was at the checkout. Of course, he recognized me. Until this moment he had always said "Hello". With shell-shocked speechlessness he noted Dad's uninviting reserve and my tear-streaked cheeks and wet pants. My humiliation was complete.

Dad and I rode home in silence. Once out of the car with the grocery bag in his arms Dad turned toward me as I got out of the car. He met my eyes for a second.

"I'm sorry," he said before shifting his gaze to look past me.

I muttered a quiet "It's alright," the safe answer, before I turned and retreated into the house, beelined to my bedroom and closed the door. No, it wasn't "alright", but I had just learned what a sassy remark would get me.

How many slaps would I have gotten for, "Did you decide you were sorry after you saw the way the clerk looked at us?"

Dad had supper ready when Mom got home. I have no recollection of what he made, nor whether I helped. I don't remember conversation around our table that night.

I have no memory of whether Carlyn was there or not. Maybe Carlyn was already away at college. The years have blurred together. Was I 14? Was I 17? Maybe I was old enough to drive. Maybe I was a self-absorbed teenager who couldn't be bothered to cook a meal. What seems most accurate to me now decades after the fact is that I was a kid who waited for instruction. Spontaneity and I were strangers.

Later that evening Mom pulled me aside and told me Dad had confessed to her what he had done. I remember very well the inappropriate smile on her face. She waited for me to say something. Was this a prompt for me to say Dad was the mean one because it was he who hit me this time? Was I supposed to apologize for having misunderstood through the years that Dad was the bad parent? There was nothing to come out of my mouth that wouldn't earn me another slap. I dipped my head and walked away without a reply.

Quitting Smoking

I'd Walk A Mile For A Camel

Former Slogan of R. J. Reynolds Tobacco Company

After the Surgeon General's first warning of the hazards of tobacco use was reported in 1964, Dad and Mom resolved to quit smoking. Because nicotine is believed by some to be one of the most addictive drugs, it's remarkable to me now that through pure determination – no patch, no Nicorette gum - Dad was able to keep his pledge. He never smoked again. Mom, on the other hand, in mere hours, lit up.

A supportive spouse who had his wife's health and best interest at heart might have spoken some words of encouragement. But neither of my parents knew how to encourage. Each harbored an irresistible need to claim accolades for her or himself in contrast to the exhibition of failure by the other.

As evening dinner ended, Mom lit a cigarette at the table, her announcement to us all that she withdrew her vow of abstinence. I don't remember Dad's precise words, but they were something like:

"So much for strength of character," which he paired with a condescending look at Mom.

Instead of admitting her weakness and asking for help, Mom knew only to bring Dad down to her level. She blew a cloud of smoke in his direction.

"If you continue to do that I'm going to go outside," he said calmly, rising from the table.

Saying nothing but smiling deviously Mom took another drag. This time she blew smoke rings directly toward Dad's face. Without another word, Dad did exactly what he said he would do and quietly walked out the back door.

Mom must have believed Dad would not be strong enough to walk away from a cigarette. She continued to smoke in silence as my sister and I got up to clear the table and wash the supper dishes. It seemed lonely to sit at the table with only a cigarette for company. I paused a moment on my way to the kitchen.

"I never knew you could blow smoke rings, Mom!"

"Oh, sure. It's really easy."

She sounded proud, and she gave us another demonstration.

Christmas Vacations

⸻ ❦ ⸻

It's time we hung some tinsel on that evergreen bough
For I've grown a little leaner
Grown a little colder
Grown a little sadder
Grown a little older
And I need a little angel
Sitting on my shoulder
Need a little Christmas now

From *We Need a Little Christmas* by Jerry Herman

A bestial moan awakened me. The motel room was dark except for a stark white light over the sink in the bathroom. Another anguished sound. It came from the floor at the foot of Mom and Dad's bed which was next to the bed my sister and I shared. I raised onto my elbows. I could make out one prone and still figure in my parents' bed. Then I saw movement on the floor, someone crawling toward the bathroom. Disheveled hair obscured the face. A tangled blanket on the floor impeded forward progress. A growl of frustration, a yank on the blanket and the person was moving again. Reaching the toilet, the individual threw back the seat with a smack and retched into the bowl. Bawling cries, the likes of which I hadn't heard since we lived on the cattle farm, came from the wretch kneeling head down, arms resting on the rim of the toilet.

Except that the sufferer appeared drunk, the person had some resemblance to my mother.

More awake I looked at my parents' bed again. The body snoring there sounded like Dad. My sister lay asleep next to me.

I stared in shock at the sick woman by the toilet. It was Mom!

Should I do something?

Only a fool would approach an unpredictable wild animal. I was no fool. Instead, I laid in bed snug in my indignity. This was the woman who informed us that everything that went wrong in our family was Dad's fault. This was the woman who visited our pastor to express despair at her husband's loss of control over drinking. This was the woman who battled like a warrior to keep from losing control of all of us.

A few minutes passed before Mom crawled back to the blanket on the floor at the foot of her bed. She moaned as she collapsed heavily on the blanket. I listened to her breathing become rhythmic. Eventually my own must have fallen into harmony.

In the morning we were back in the cold car resuming our drive to Kansas on Christmas vacation. Dad's cousin Ruby's rural bar and motel disappeared behind us on a curve of Nebraska highway. The car windows were frosty. So was my judgmental silence.

When Mom pressed me to know what my sullen teenage attitude was about, I spit out the words, "I saw you crawling across the floor drunk last night."

"I wasn't drunk! I was sick!"

"Uh huh."

My skepticism provoked her. Her anger began a slow smolder. It was several years before it ignited. When it finally did, I was a freshman at the University of Minnesota, home on Christmas break. Carlyn was home for the holidays, too, from Bemidji State. Carlyn accepted an invitation from her high school boyfriend's sister for the two of us to come to a Christmas party while we were home. We sisters ascended a wooden staircase in an alley behind Spring Valley's main street. We followed footprints in the snow up un-shoveled steps that were illuminated by a streetlamp. Under the close supervision of our parents neither my sister nor I had ever partied while we were in high school. Drinking was a new experience. That evening I became an earnest apprentice.

Liquor bottles crowded the counter of the apartment's small kitchen. Eager to demonstrate that I had gained worldliness at college, I accepted a beer from one of the guests. It went down rapidly despite the bitterness. The taste wasn't the point. The appearance of sophistication was what I was after, though I'm sure I had the allure of a smiling sophisticate with a spinach leaf stuck on an incisor.

In addition to the polished veneer of a beer swilling debutante, the beer gave me a divine loss of self-consciousness. It empowered me. When one of the young men at the party offered another drink, I didn't hesitate.

"Say, you're Officer Erion's daughter, aren't you?" the fellow asked me with a sly smile.

"Yes," I answered, sensing - but deliberately ignoring - the possibility of malevolent intentions.

"I'll make you something special."

What a gentleman! Whatever he gave me went down as easily as soda pop. He watched closely while I drank. Some of his friends also took interest in my enjoyment of the head-spinning sweet concoction. They were attentive and wouldn't allow my glass to sit empty. Carelessly, I enjoyed feeling like a guy magnate. It seemed like the party was just getting started when Carlyn interrupted my fun.

"It's time to go."

When I stood up the room tilted. Carlyn stuffed my arms into the sleeves of my coat and steered me out the door to the pitching exterior staircase. There was laughter behind me as I sat in the snow and bumped down the steps on my butt while Carlyn grasped the back of my coat collar.

She helped me into the car and began to drive.

"Slow down!" I ordered as I watched the shoulder of the road whoosh by at a nauseating 20-miles an hour.

At 15-miles an hour it must have taken a long time to get home, especially because Carlyn pulled over several times to allow me to be sick in the ditch. The drive home was nothing, though, compared to the trip from the front door to our bedroom.

Mom was like a drug-dog. She was off the couch before the door closed behind me. She homed in on my unsteady gait and the inebriated smile on my face. Pressing her canine-like nose close to me she seemed determined to ferret out all the informative clues.

"Who's drunk now?" she demanded as I slid along the wall of the hallway toward the bedroom.

I was relieved the question was rhetorical because my tongue was paralyzed. Nevertheless, with Mom hovering near, I could conceal nothing about my condition. I fell on my back on my bed and closed my eyes while Mom drilled Carlyn about our activities.

The next thing I can now recall was Carlyn bringing me to consciousness as she wiped my face.

"Come to the bathroom so we can get you cleaned up," she said patiently.

"Just leave her like she is," I heard Mom say, disgust in her voice. "That will teach her a lesson."

"What's going on?" I asked dimly.

"You threw up on yourself," Carlyn answered. Although Carlyn may not have been aware of the danger of suffocation, I have since heard tragic stories of drunks dying of suffocating in their own puke. I owe my life to my sister for ignoring Mom's advice.

The next morning, I was full of chagrin as I received from Mom exactly what I treated her to on the Christmas trip to Kansas: disgusted glares, angry sighs, and disapproving judgment. My self-awareness wouldn't allow me to deny my folly. I knew I deserved the consequences.

∼

Whist Night

"Life shrinks or expands in proportion to one's courage."

Anais Nin

One weeknight as we lingered around the supper table after our meal, an impulsive idea struck Dad like a smack to the head.

"Let's ask Thor and Audrey over for Whist tonight," he said to Mom.

Whist was their go-to card game when my parents had two players besides themselves. It didn't baffle me that my sister and I had never been invited to play. What puzzled me more was the sight of a dad participating in a ball-toss with his son as I passed their yard. A parent playing with their children was foreign to me.

"I have a test tomorrow, Dad," said Carlyn as she got up to help clear the table.

Mom said nothing as she snubbed out her cigarette and exhaled a lungful of smoke across the table. Spent from a day at the factory, she got up and crossed to the living room where she picked up the Rochester Post Bulletin and plopped on the couch. The newspaper's crossword puzzle gave Mom magical powers. With it she could deflect present circumstances. She wouldn't have to pick a side in this discussion if she focused on Twelve Across.

Dad ignored Carlyn. He got up from the table and went to the wall phone. As he picked up the receiver to dial our former neighbors, Carlyn swirled past him and stomped down the hall toward our bedroom.

"I have to study!"

Dad slammed the receiver in its cradle and followed her. From the table where I stacked plates, I saw him step into our bedroom and grab Carlyn by the shoulder. He spun her around with one hand while he shoved our bedroom door closed with the other. I heard sharp smacks and shouting.

"Who do you think you're walking away from?"

"It's not fair to us when you have a party on a school night!"

I glanced at Mom who nestled against the arm of the couch with her folded newspaper. She looked up at me from her crossword puzzle with a hint of guilt in her eyes.

"I always told your father if he ever laid a hand on either of you girls, I would leave him."

I grimaced and gave my head a slight shake, which is as close as a coward could come to asking if that was the only solution.

At that, Mom perked up. My head bobble had absolved her. There were still angry voices down the hall, but she smiled.

Weeks later I overheard Mom defend herself to a friend saying that leaving the man would be too upsetting to her daughters.

When Dad strode back from the bedroom the only clue that something had changed was that he passed the phone without pausing. He yanked open the refrigerator door and pulled out a Grain Belt. I heard the satisfying snap of the cap which fell to the counter. No one said a word. Not Dad. Not me. Not Mom who had resumed studying Twelve Across.

I ducked down the hall where I found Carlyn standing in the middle of our room like a bulwark. If her fierce expression was any indication, the red color on her cheeks was as much from anger as slaps. There were no tears. She had defied Dad effectively. We should have high-fived each other. Instead, I crept back to the kitchen and washed the dishes. Afterward, I went downstairs to the corner of our concrete block basement I claimed for my schoolwork. I picked up a textbook from the card table and sat down on a folding chair. Now, if only the book would give me magical powers like the crossword puzzle gave Mom.

Magical Potions

· ❧ ·

"When you can stop you don't want to. And when you
want to stop you can't. That's addiction."

Quote from HealthyPlace.com

*I did have magical potions, though. At the age of 13 I discovered that
graham crackers bestow magical powers in the very first bite … or even before
the first bite while I'm still pouring the whole milk over the bowl of crumbled
crackers. No. Even sooner. When I stop fighting the urge. When I surrender.
Before I pull the bowl out of the cupboard. Before I open the box of graham
crackers and rip open the wax paper. Before I stand in the chill of the open
refrigerator door in search of the milk.*

*In the moment I give myself permission there's a euphoric power surge. I
swear I could lift a car. I feel giddy and guilty simultaneously. I know I'm going
to regret this, but I'm powerless anyway and therefore, relieved. There's nothing
to be done, so I may as well enjoy this.*

*But I must stay in the moment. In this one miniscule moment loneliness
and inadequacy vanish. In the next moment I will care, so this one must never
end. In this moment of ecstasy, culpability is postponed.*

*I stand over the kitchen sink with a bowl in one hand and a spoon in the
other, and all I know, all I am aware of, is the sweet taste of the mushy crackers
and the soft moans that seem to be coming from …me! I raise the bowl to my
lips and slurp the dregs of sweet milk.*

*I crumble more crackers into the bowl and drown them in more milk. The
crackers must have no hard edges. They must soothe like a poultice. They must
ease the wounds of insufficiency. I plunge my spoon into the thick mush and
lift a dripping mouthful to my salivating mouth.*

*When my bowl is empty again, I have a third. I have to. The moments
must string together as long as possible to ward off the self-loathing that lies at*

the bottom of the bowl. No matter how gorged I feel, I keep refilling the bowl until the graham cracker box is empty, or until the magic flees at the sound of Mom's car tires on the gravel driveway.

Every time the aura vanishes, I am left more abashed than I was before. The only recourse I know is to assuage myself in this same way at the very next opportunity.

Sex

"Boundaries aren't all bad. That's why there are
walls around mental institutions."

Peggy Noonan

"Kathy, come in here and pick up this towel," Mom called from the bedroom.

What am I, the maid? I grumbled silently to my 17-year old self as I walked obediently to my parents' closed bedroom door.

They were ordinarily early risers, even on weekend mornings like this, so it surprised me when I opened the door and saw Mom still in bed. I heard Dad across the hall in the bathroom. The covers were pulled up to Mom's bare shoulders. Her hair was topsy-turvy, but her smile was exultant. I returned her smile with a scowl to let her know I was being inconvenienced. I surveyed their room.

"What towel?"

"It's on the floor over there," she said pointing to Dad's side of the bed.

I stepped around the foot of their bed and saw a bath towel in a heap on the floor.

What's the big emergency that this single towel must be picked up right now by me? I asked only in my thoughts.

I reached down for it.

"Don't touch it!" Mom hollered with alarm, even though a jubilant smile was on her face.

I stopped and looked at the towel, then looked back at Mom.

"How can I pick it up if I can't touch it?"

"Just be careful," she cautioned delightedly.

I wasn't going to ask, "Be careful of what?" because a revelation came to me in that moment. I picked up the corner of the towel with my thumb and index finger and dragged it from the room without another word or look at Mom. As I walked down the basement steps to the laundry still dragging the towel, I understood Mom just announced to me that she and Dad had sex.

What I didn't understand was why. Did she think I would give her kudos? I didn't know a single thing about their marital intimacies, and even that was more than I ever wanted to know. Now, if I had been a normal teenager with a circle of girlfriends who shared secrets, I might have taken this detail to them for a squeamish howl. Lacking that, and my sister who was away at college, I let my reaction (Are you kidding me?!) fester.

Before the day was over, I sneaked into the kitchen, took a spoon from the drawer and a jar of peanut butter from the fridge.

~

Banshees

Be farther than an arm-length from your parent if you decide to sass.

Kate Erion

We were home alone when Mom reached out and slapped my face for a disrespectful remark I made. What the remark was I can't remember, but that it was disrespectful I have no doubt. We were a family inured to disrespect. None of us was happy, and it was always someone else's fault. It was de rigueur to inform the offending party of their perceived role in our woefulness.

"I could be happy if you didn't drink!"

"I could be happy if you weren't fat!"

"I could be happy if you two weren't yelling at each other all the time!" And so on.

Something had been building in me long before that moment of contact. Self-pity, more than likely. Anger, of course. A sense of injustice, certainly, because this was the 1960's and the justice of everything was up for debate."

At church we were admonished to keep the commandments. "Honor your father and your mother." Had no one figured out that you get what you give? Some say it is possible to be respectful to the person who is disrespectful to you, but I hadn't learned yet how to do that.

"Thou shalt not kill." Why was anyone surprised, that some Americans asked publicly about the morality of sending young men to Viet Nam to kill and be killed? College was attainable for more young people than ever before in the history of our country. Why should women be limited to only the study of nursing or teaching? If a woman was interested in the subjects of economics, engineering, or architecture, why shouldn't she pursue those careers? If all people were truly equal, why weren't they all treated the same?

When Mom slapped me, my right hand reached up in a reflexive retaliation and whacked Mom hard on her left cheek. I remember her look. It probably mirrored my own: shocked self-righteousness. Red-faced, she hit me again. I lifted my hand to give her another cuff, but she grabbed me by the wrist.

"You aren't supposed to do that," she said in breathless astonishment.

I struggled to free my hand as I retorted, "YOU aren't supposed to do that!"

Our eyes locked, and we strained in a combative embrace. Mom believed to her soul that she had every right to use corporal punishment on her children. It was a common concept. I was aware that the adage "spare the rod; spoil the child" was being elbowed aside by alternative child-rearing philosophies, but those new ideologies were taking a long time to filter down to this family.

As we struggled my confidence faded. What would I do if I won this fight? I loosened my grip. Mom slapped me one more time to demonstrate her authority and we stepped apart in a stalemate - not a truce.

A week later for a minor infraction she slapped my face again with a masterful expression that said God, the Law and the PTA authorized her to do so. The murderous look I gave her was not meant to intimidate. It was the actual intention of my feelings. If I had had a weapon at that instant, I would have killed her with no remorse. She never hit me again.

Seeking

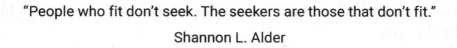

"People who fit don't seek. The seekers are those that don't fit."

Shannon L. Alder

In my freshman year of college, I struggled for normalcy. I believed there was one normal way to be, and I had to find it. I had trouble making friends because I was wary of everyone. If I didn't behave appropriately, I feared I would be ridiculed, rejected, and left friendless. To alleviate being shunned, I kept to myself. That logic didn't even eliminate the ridicule because I ridiculed myself. Authority figures always knew what was best for me, so I sought out a psychiatrist through the University Health Service. The psych department gave me the MMPI and an appointment with a graduate student to go over the test results.

I entered the graduate student's silent office where a tiny woman only a few years older than myself sat behind a giant desk in a near empty room. Tall unshaded windows behind her allowed gray outside light to illuminate the stark desktop on which was one manila folder. It had my name on it. The woman did not get up. She did not greet me. She did not smile.

"Please sit down," she said in a serious tone that worried me. What was the diagnosis? Would it result in electric shock therapy?

Without speaking I sat rigidly in a chair across the desk from her waiting for the bad news.

She opened the folder and scanned the few papers inside. "Your test results show there is nothing wrong with you," she said.

I waited for the "But...". It took me over two hours to take the damn test. Certainly, she was going to say more.

She looked up at me. "You are normal."

"OK", I answered drawing out the "a" sound in a questioning tone.

Then, after a pause, "You are sane," she said.

"Alright." Still, I waited.

"Yes," she said with a sober nod as she closed the file.

She said nothing more.

Oh! I understood. The appointment was over.

"Thank you?" I said standing slowly enough that she could stop me before I left the room if she decided to say more.

But she did not speak up, look up or get up. I turned and left her sitting behind the fortification of her desk. The only sound was the click of the door latch as I exited. Walking back to the dorm I had much to think about. Apparently, it is normal to feel diffident and alone. I could be happy in my unhappiness because it was normal.

A person should never stop trying to make sense of their situation, right? Maybe a theologian would offer more insight.

Mom's family was full of ordained ministers. I think every single one of Grandpa Stern's brothers (in a family with 14 births) was an ordained minister for the Church of the Brethren. It would not be a stretch that at least one of Grandpa's sons would also attend the seminary. That one was Uncle Paul. In the 1960s Uncle Paul left the Church of the Brethren and joined the Bahá'I Faith. He carried his new religion to Japan and lived there, preaching it, for many years. Based on his studies, background and beliefs it was no surprise that he asked me once what my own belief was regarding Jesus Christ. I felt honored that he cared to know what I thought. I told him I believed there really was a Jesus, but I believed Him to be a human being, a mortal, a man, and a child of God only as much as the rest of us.

"Wrong!" said Uncle Paul.

He then proceeded to tell me Jesus was at the very least a chosen profit with loftier insight than mere human beings. When he began listing the prophets and what each had contributed, I realized with disappointment that Uncle Paul's inquiry of my belief was simply his method of opening his instructional sermon to me.

Prior to that lecture I had written to Uncle Paul while he was spreading the teachings of Bahá'ulláh. I thought this scholarly theologian and member of the inner sanctum of my mother's family might have some insights to share about what could be done to improve my relationships. I decided that specific issue was the one to tackle, because I didn't realize the first relationship to improve upon was the relationship with myself. Away the airmail letter went and before long I received an airmail letter back. Uncle Paul penned me a reprimand for not heeding Christianity's 5th Commandment: "Thou shalt honor thy father and thy mother." End of discussion.

I bristled. It would be easier to honor them if I felt they honored me! I threw away every Japanese rice bowl, carving and piece of bamboo Uncle Paul ever sent me. I would never again seek help from "no stinkin' theologian!"

~

Foster Girls

"The fundamental love of your family allows
you to expose your vulnerabilities."

Doris Kearns Goodwin

Because Mom and Dad succeeded in getting their daughters through high school with relatively good grades and without pregnancies or other scandals, they congratulated themselves on being excellent parents. Feeling good about themselves they decided to become a foster home for four female juvenile offenders at the beginning of my senior year in high school. Certainly, part of the motivation to take on this challenge was to help pay for their daughters' college tuition. Another part was altruistic. They believed their stern version of parenting was good parenting. I'm sure they presumed that troubled young girls everywhere secretly yearned for strict discipline.

Adding four young strangers with issues to a family is guaranteed to create a shift. Carlyn was already away at Bemidji State. If I felt alone at home, Carlyn must have felt completely forgotten. She wouldn't say she felt abandoned, but she admitted that if she ever had been prone to depression, it was during her years at college 300 miles from home.

As the actual daughter and the oldest in this group home I should have had special status. I had never been convicted of a crime, I was not at risk for running away, my schoolwork was above average, and I had a driver's license. However, if a rule was established for the girls, it applied to me as well. The United States' military was Dad's model. In the first summer he rousted all of us, even Mom, out of bed in the mornings to jog a mile down the shoulder of Highways 16/63. I don't know why he didn't keep up the regimen. Maybe it occurred to him that most of these girls – and Mom – smoked, and that he was the only one who knew how to do CPR. Maybe it occurred to him that the shoulder of a highway where 18-wheelers roared past us at 60 mph wasn't the safest place for a work-out. Or maybe it was just too much work to enforce the regimen. The copious complaints might have worn Dad down. The entire regimen was scrapped in less than a month.

I did intend to be an inspiring example of obedient behavior, a paragon of virtue, to these girls, but I'm sure they mostly thought I was ridiculous. I could have been a friend if I had known how to be one. But these would have been friendships with sanctions. Mom allowed no free-lancing. It was one thing to accept Sandy's offer to pierce my ears, but it was a totally different matter to be a confidant to Joanne. Mom's daughter wasn't going to fraternize with "her girls". When I left for college in the fall, I wrote what I intended to be an encouraging letter to Joanne saying I knew her living situation was "no bed of roses". What I thought I was saying was that however challenging her stint at our house was, it was survivable. Mom read my letter to Joanne, with or without permission. I don't know which. On my next visit home Mom told me to sit at the dining table with her and the foster girls.

"Tell Jo that what you meant by 'bed of roses' was in regard to her court-ordered detention away from her family," Mom ordered. "It was not about our family's rules," she scripted for me.

Way to put a girl in an awkward spot, Mom! Both Joanne and I knew that wasn't my meaning, but I didn't have the courage to be honest with my bristling Mother as she presided over the confession in front of the foster girls. When I spoke the words Mom told me to say, Joanne stood up abruptly and fled to the basement where her bedroom was. There ended the potential for a friendship. Joanne was betrayed, and I was ashamed. I realize as I write this that I never did make an amend to Joanne. I owe her one.

Dad had built bedrooms in our basement for the girls. He also installed a shower for them and a chemical toilet. Every morning after the girls left for school Dad emptied their toilet. One weekend when I was home from college, it occurred to Dad that instead of running the gauntlet of teenage girls himself on a Saturday morning, he would have me collect their toilet.

Ooogah! Ooogah! Breach! Breach! A penetrating alarm went off in my head.

"You can't be serious! I will not!"

"Yes, you will!"

He had that same firm set to his jaw and that glint in his eyes he had the day he slapped me and took me grocery shopping. Mom stood at the kitchen sink washing breakfast dishes and listening to this argument. I looked at her. She said nothing. I knew what Dad was capable of, and I had no ally. I wasn't allowed to speak frankly to the girls, but I could be drafted to be the girls' janitor. Which humiliation would be worse: the humiliation of being the foster girls' janitor, or the humiliation of Dad slapping me? I folded.

The girls relished it! Their cat calls began as soon as my feet touched the basement floor.

"Ha, Ha! Look who's here to haul our shit!"

"Kathy's doing a shitty job!"

"Don't spill any on ya'!"

I was lonely at college and suffered indignity at home. I hated my life. I hated myself. Sometimes I would think how satisfying it would be if I could simply quit life. Lingering on that thought was like turning a black and white scene into a color image, and that was too vivid for my sensibilities. Hating myself was familiar and natural, but a violent act against myself would be frightening and painful. What were my options? The only alternative was to be better, re-make myself. Begin a self-improvement campaign. There was a book on the bookshelf above the piano called *How to Win Friends and Influence People* [7]by Dale Carnegie (Carnegie). Mom said it was Dad's book, but I had never seen him read it. He wouldn't miss it. I slipped it into my suitcase when I went back to college. Maybe this had the answers I hoped for.

Dream

"I am following my dreams to prove my nightmares wrong."

Synthia Beauvais

The paved highway is a narrow two-lane with no shoulders. It is built on a gravel reef that crosses the middle of a deep lake. The highway is 20 feet above the surface of the rippling icy water. Gravel planes steeply down from the pavement. There are no guard rails, no wide spots to pull over. Nevertheless, it is imperative that I turn the black four-door sedan around. I don't know why, but we must go back. My four women passengers, three in the backseat, one in the front seat with me, argue.

Two say, "Go all the way across and come back."

Two say, "It's too far. You have to go back now."

I agonize over which is the best decision. Ours is the only vehicle on the highway. The car is as long as the road is wide, but I believe I can safely maneuver the vehicle around. I slow the low-slung sedan and nose it into the opposite lane. If I pull too far forward the tires will go off the pavement and onto the steeply pitched gravel. I inch the vehicle forward, turning the steering wheel tightly. The front tires kiss the gravel. I put the car in reverse and turn the wheel in the opposite direction. Slowly the sedan moves back until I hear the back tires crunch on the gravel. I shift into drive and press my foot carefully against the accelerator. The back tires start to spin. I take my foot off the accelerator and straighten the wheel. Gently I press the peddle again. The tires spin. I shift into reverse and allow the vehicle to move back a couple of inches to find a more secure purchase lower on the embankment, but even with my foot on the brake the car continues to roll backward. Shouting, my passengers fling open their doors, but the slope and the speed intimidate. No one jumps out. The sedan rolls back, and its tailpipe submerges. Everyone screams as the vehicle rolls into the lake carrying all of us with it.

I wake with a gasp and bolt upright in bed.

Distressed I scold myself for choosing wrongly. Why didn't I drive to the opposite side before turning around?

My palms are damp. My heart pounds. It was a dream, just a dream I tell myself. Blessed relief flows into me.

~

PART II

A Fine Kettle of Fish

New Worlds

It's been so long, it's been so long, a little too long
A change has gotta come

From A Change Is Gonna Come by Sam Cooke

All in all, 1968 was quite a year. Among many other headlines, the North Vietnamese shocked the United States with a devasting New Year attack in January that left more Americans asking for facts about the war in Viet Nam. In March the US Army perpetrated war crimes by killing hundreds of Vietnamese people in the My Lai Massacre. Also in March, beleaguered President Johnson announced he would not seek reelection. In April Martin Luther King, Jr. was assassinated. Race riots began then. The same month the Civil Rights Act was signed into law. In June Senator Robert Kennedy was assassinated. In August race riots occurred during the Democratic National Convention in Chicago.

Our champions of a better world, Dr. Martin Luther King Junior and Robert Kennedy were dedicated to moral causes, including civil rights.

I don't remember Dad saying anything about civil rights. Though it seemed reasonable to me that a member of one minority might welcome equality for all minorities, to take a stand a person might call attention to himself. Then he might have to answer questions he'd rather not discuss about his own heritage.

Dad did, however, express an opinion on the war.

"If you are called, you go."

So it went without saying, if your parents tell you, "You are going to college", you go to college. I didn't mind the idea of college, but I had no idea what I was going to do there. I was under-exposed to life when I was delivered to the door of the dormitory Pioneer Hall on the University of

Minnesota campus at the end of the summer. My little life felt as uncertain as life anywhere else in the world that year. It seemed that I should be glad to begin taking charge of my life for the first time, but I had no idea what to do with it. Besides, I didn't have much experience in choosing correctly.

~

The University of Minnesota

I can't decide
I don't know
Which Way to go?
The more you learn
The less you know

From *Fiction* by Joni Mitchell

My luggage was bursting with self-doubt. I understood obedience, but other people had different thoughts. Cassius Clay, for instance, made a good opposing argument to the war:

"We are not supposed to take part in no wars unless declared by Allah …"

Hmm. That sounded a lot like what Grandpa and Grandma Stern said: "Thou shalt not kill."

And Dad's advice to become a teacher left me wondering, "Teach what?" Teach kids to follow "the path"? Is there one path? There seemed to be so many. And I myself had never managed to choose the correct one. How would I be able to recommend a path to anyone?

On a cloudy day during orientation week we freshmen were provided a tour of the University's St. Paul campus. A University spokesman told the 40 or 50 of us who packed into a machine shed to get out of the rain, something like a mere 60% of us would graduate. I had no hope. If I had any idea what else to do besides what I was told to do, I would have packed up and left the day it was confirmed that my chances were slim to none.

But I didn't have any idea, so I stayed, not thinking much past midterms and finals. A little corner grocery store that students nick-named "Dirty Roy's" a couple of blocks from my dorm helped me cope. After dinners in the dormitory cafeteria, I'd walk over to Dirty Roy's and choose between a package of powdered doughnuts or a package of glazed doughnuts, or if I had the cash, one of each, for dessert.

One thing did thrill me. I volunteered to be an usher at the University's Northrup Auditorium. The only thing volunteers had to do was to show up before the performances in black skirts and white blouses and show guests to their seats. Ushers got to watch every show we worked for free, which was a bargain even if we had to stand for the entire presentation. The evening the house lights dimmed, and the Royal Ballet danced onto the stage was spellbinding. I stood in the dark against the back wall with all my muscles tensing as in my imagination I stepped every step with the troupe. When the audience stood and applauded Dame Margot Fonteyn for what – in my foolish youth – I took to be a lackluster solo, I did not appreciate that she was 50 years old at the time. Nevertheless, collectively the Royal Ballet enchanted me. After the performance I leaped, twirled and spun all the way back to the dormitory, dreaming the what-if without a clue that all I lacked was belief in myself.

Despite not declaring a major, every quarter at the University I enrolled in a Spanish class. Spring Valley High School had an excellent Spanish language teacher who turned me on to dreaming of far-away places. Each time I went to the University's language lab I had reveries beneath breathtaking posters taped to the walls. Gîza, Machu Pichu, Neuschwanstein.

During winter quarter of my freshman year a pretty, blonde Spanish instructor not even a decade older than me showed us slides of her trip to Chile. There were several slides of Chilean policemen helping her cut yellow flowers from a tree. In the final slide the policemen's jeep was filled with tree branches dripping in blossoms. The teacher, her friends and the officers crowded around the jeep laughing in amusement in the cheerful sunlight. The slide looked like another travel poster, and I wanted to be with her in that picture. No. I wanted to be her in that picture.

A couple of weeks later when that Spanish class was visited by an exchange group from the YMCA in Santiago, Chile, I went straight to the University's campus YMCA and inquired how to get into the exchange program headed for Chile. It was the first thing I did with certainty at the

U. I was given an appointment for an interview. In less than a week I took a phone call from the Y telling me I was one of 20 students accepted into the Chilean Exchange Program. I called my unaware parents and stunned them with my announcement that I was going to Chile.

Chile

I was so afraid Fernando
We were young and full of life and none of us prepared to die
And I'm not ashamed to say
The roar of guns and cannons almost made me cry

From *Fernando* by Benny Andersson and Bjoern Ulvaeus

Never had I decided on my own what to do, and then, voila, had the wish granted – or worked to make it happen. But the next thing I knew I was on a Lan Chile airline on my way to Santiago. The summer of 1969 while I was literally out of my world, there were others who were literally out of the world. I lived with the gracious Fermandois, my host family comprised of a widow and her three adult children. We gathered shoulder to shoulder on their couch in front of their black and white television on July 20 and watched Neil Armstrong step onto the surface of our moon. The irony struck me that the day before I had watched a man drive a donkey cart loaded with firewood down a dirt road outside of Santiago.

The YMCA sent auditory testing machines with us exchange students to test the hearing of children at a boys' orphanage run by the National Police Force. We Americans went to the orphanage on weekdays to test the kids' hearing, to play with them and to help with other chores like mending their clothes.

As a thank you, the National Police Force treated us to a banquet on the orphanage grounds shortly after the moon landing. It was a generous mid-day affair in one of the barracks where our hosts had set up a long, elegant table covered with white linens. Each place setting had a charger plate, a cloth napkin, silverware and a wine glass. We feasted on innumerable delicious courses, two of which I remember included porotos granados, their native dish of beans, and a meat pie with ground corn in place of a pie crust, pastel de choclo. All through the meal our hosts kept our glasses full of hearty red wine from a Chilean winery, Concha Y Toro.

When all the food had been consumed one of our hosts stood and raised a glass to the helpful American students. We all drank to that. Then another of our hosts proposed a toast to Apollo 11. We all drank to that, too. Someone else toasted to Apollo 12. By the time we drank a toast to Apollo 20 our arms were linked all the way around the table. We sang happy songs that we learned as we drank. Joy filled me. I was part of a circle of laughing, singing, warm people. I felt as content and included as a baby in the warm embrace of a parent.

On the toast to Apollo 25 hosts and guests alike swayed from side to side in rhythm with the songs, our arms still linked. As I swayed right, I was pulled left by a petite dark-haired uniformed woman who was stronger than she looked. I lost my balance and tipped out of the chair, crashing onto the floor and laughing hilariously. It was wonderful to feel so carefree. The kind officer helped me up and, clutching my hand, towed me to the ladies' room where she ran cold water on my wrists - as if I were drunk when I was merely happy. Or so I told myself. I let her minister to me if she thought she should. She was a trained guardian, after all.

I left Santiago the way I left everything - with a certainty that I would not be missed; that I was inconsequential to my hosts. To that end, I kept no ties to people and places behind me. It saddens me now, because the good people of Chile went through horrific trauma in the years following my visit. They elected a Marxist president, Salvador Allende, in 1970. His election must have thrilled Oscar, the novio of one of the Fermandois daughters, who had unabashedly announced to me that he was a "communisto". Allende's first year was favorable, and this awesome little country was something to hold in high regard. But the United States government didn't like Marxists. They didn't approve of the success of Marxists. Our government also didn't like that Allende had meddled with United States' mining interests in Chile. In retaliation the United States meddled with Allende. In covert tactics involving the CIA Chile was quickly brought to economic shambles, and a deranged military man opposed to "communistos", Augusto Pinochet, was elected after Allende committed suicide. Years of torture, outright murder, imprisonment and exile tore thousands of Chilean families asunder. I covered my ears and tried not to think about what had become of Oscar and the Fermandois family.

~

Scuba Diving

Sittin' here resting my bones
And this loneliness won't leave me alone
It's two thousand miles I roamed
Just to make this dock my home

From *(Sittin' On) The Dock of the Bay* by Otis Redding

The weight of a 30-pound air tank on my back and a lead belt around my waist counteracted the natural buoyancy of my body. At first, though, it was hard to tell if I was drifting down, floating up, or if I remained at the same depth, weight and buoyancy balancing each other out. Was I sinking or were the rising bubbles creating an optical illusion? The sunlit surface didn't seem to be distancing rapidly. I kicked with my swim fins a couple of times to see if I rose toward the surface. There! I rose with the bubbles. When I stopped kicking, I could detect that I, indeed, descended.

I looked around for my diving buddy, Laura. Her enthusiasm for this sport infused me. I met her while I worked as a janitor in Pioneer Hall. She talked me into taking scuba lessons and getting certified. It was fun in the controlled environment of a swimming pool. The class emphasis on safety made me think about things I hadn't initially considered. I didn't share Laura's verve now that we were on our way to see the bottom of Cass Lake, 120 ear-crushing feet below us.

Laura propelled herself head-first toward the black nothingness. She was a careful diver and looked back for me. We waved at each other, but I didn't swim toward her. She swam back up to my depth. We looked down together at the inscrutable darkness below the reach of the sun. We hadn't thought to bring lights.

I could barely hear the just discernable hum of Dad's outboard motor fading away toward the shore above the sound of my deep breaths pulling air through the regulator. Dad had delivered us to the deepest point of the lake, as asked. What more was there for him to do? We hadn't asked for anything else. We were adults. Adults don't require supervision. Mom and Dad had company coming that evening. He had to get back and make sure there was enough beer chilling.

The hazards spoke louder than the promised adventure. I motioned to Laura that I was going to pull the cord to inflate my vest. She nodded and we pulled our cords simultaneously. Up we glided.

Should we return to shore swimming below the water on SCUBA? It seemed safer to swim on the surface to keep an eye out for boats, but swimming with inflated vests and weight belts is not ideal. We couldn't stretch out over the water to take effective strokes with our arms. Our equipment was designed to keep our heads up and our butts down even with fins on our kicking feet. We relied on the wind as much as on our arms and legs to propel ourselves over the surface of the water, but the wind was not stiff that afternoon. Nor was it direct. What wind there was blew us northerly despite our efforts to swim east.

The sun was down by the time we staggered onto the beach. Nearly full tanks feel weightless in the water. On shore we felt every pound. Still, it seemed practical to carry the tanks on our backs rather than remove them and carry them in our arms. We couldn't have moved faster if we had taken our tanks off and pulled them through thigh high water along the shore.

We had a half mile walk to Mom and Dad's home. Lights were on inside the house, and we could hear laughter and the slap of cards on the plywood "table". Laura and I let our tank straps slide off our aching shoulders. We pitched ourselves on the grass where we dropped our fins, masks and weight belts.

"Let's go around to the garage and change out of our suits," I suggested. Our bunk beds were in the garage. Mom and Dad's new house here was still under construction. It was Dad's dream to retire on a lake where he could fish to his heart's content. I don't think he realized when he dreamed about his retirement that alcohol would not let him put fishing ahead of it.

"We had better let your folks know we're back. They must be worried sick," Laura recommended. I couldn't imagine them worrying, but it was polite to humor Laura.

We went in through the lake-side door where Mom and Dad sat with their friends at the make-shift table. Cards were scattered among bottles of beer and whiskey glasses. A ribbon of smoke rose from Mom's cigarette in an ashtray near her elbow.

"We're back," I announced.

Dad gave us a vacant glance.

"It's your deal, Ruth," he said.

One of their friends said, "Give me some good cards this time, Ruth."

"I gave you good cards last time. You have to play them right," she countered.

No one asked what took us so long to get back. No one asked us what the bottom of Cass Lake looked like, which was just as well, since we couldn't answer that. No one said anything to us as we passed through to the back door.

It's hard to orient yourself sometimes. People insist they love you.

If I had known then that I get what I give, I would have pulled a chair up to the table and asked them who was winning.

~

Drop Out

There is no way to take the danger out of human relationships.

Barbara Grizzuti Harrison

In my fourth year at the University where I was still undecided about whether to major in architecture, botany, journalism, philosophy, physical education, psychology, or Spanish, my friends began to explore job options, apply to graduate school, become engaged. A feeling of abandonment came over me. They were leaving me.

There was no magnetic pull from home for Christmas. I stayed at school during break to make money cleaning dorm rooms. I was content during the daytime working with a student crew, but in the evenings, I felt the solitude. My friends had gone home for the holidays.

One evening I called Uncle Willis' house in St. Louis Park, which was two city bus connections from my dorm. Dad's brother and his family always welcomed me when I managed to catch the correct buses to their house. I was surprised when my cousin Norman answered the phone. The third of six kids, he was eight years older than me. Easily two hundred pounds, taller than six feet with jet black hair, he was a substantial figure of a man. There was something in his mirthless smile that said not to trust him anymore than I would trust a deadly black mamba, but I never paid attention to my Spidey sense.

"We should hang out together some time."

I forget which one of us suggested this to the other, but just like that we settled on the upcoming Saturday night. I didn't have any expectations of what we would do. As long as I had company, it didn't really matter to me what we did.

When Norm picked me up at the dorm it was cold and dark outside.

He suggested we drive across the river to the West Bank where there was a bar he liked. To me, bars were all the same: windowless, smoke-choked, loud places patronized only by compulsive alcoholics, exuberant extroverts or troubled introverts. I guess I fit into one of those categories because I agreed to go. Norm bought the Pabst. After a couple of them – I wasn't keeping an exact count - he told me his ex-wife woes. I giggled or gasped companionably depending on who did what to whom in his story. Other than that, I don't remember my own contributions to the conversation, although I'm sure I talked about myself as attention starved people tend to do. And of course, I wanted to give the impression that I had my life under control. It must have taken a couple of hours to convey that everything was copesetic because on one of Norm's trips to the bar for more refreshments I counted the empty bottles crowding our little round table.

My first thought was, Man, Norm can really put away the beer! But then it dawned on me that he wasn't drinking alone. Half of those bottles were mine!

"The bartender is staring at you," Norm said, returning to the table with more beer.

I looked over my shoulder and recognized an exchange student from the men's side of my dormitory wiping off the bar after the departure of some patrons. I waved at him, but all I got back was a scowl. It was the kind of scowl a parent might give a child whose behavior needed correction.

Taking his cue, I said, "When we finish these we should go. I need to get back to the dorm before curfew."

"I hate to tell you this, but you already missed curfew. It's 11:00 PM."

I could have sworn that curfew was midnight on Saturdays, but the rules must have been different during quarter break.

Oh, oh!

He read my expression.

"Don't worry about it. You can come home with me for the night, and I'll bring you back in the morning."

I hesitated.

"You'll be fine if you don't mind sleeping on my couch," he offered casually.

We drank our beer and stood up to go. I glanced at the bartender who looked away then shook his head.

Was that head shake for me? Couldn't have been. I disregarded it.

At his house Norm invited me to have a seat on the couch while he turned on lights and the TV and then plopped down so close to me that I laughed.

"Are you close enough, Lover Boy?" I asked with what I thought was a tone of cool sarcasm belying my unease. I started to scoot over.

He reached toward me as if to pull me back, but instead he shocked me by pulling up the front of my sweater. Whether it was deliberate or not, he snagged my bra at the same time and exposed my left breast. I was embarrassed, but too drunk to be mortified, and trying too hard to be cool that I couldn't express outrage.

"Was that good for you?" I asked, hoping he'd catch the sarcasm while I adjusted my clothing.

Norm stood and went upstairs. I expected he'd return with a pillow and a blanket, but I fell asleep waiting.

I woke with a crushing weight pinning me to the couch. My eyes flicked open and I realized the load pressing the air out of me was Norm. My panties were pulled down, and he was trying to force his flaccid self inside of me. More terrified than revolted, I snapped my eyes shut.

Near panic because I couldn't breathe, I had to move. I yawned and stretched as if I were awakening. He yanked up my underwear and pulled down my skirt. I gasped for air but didn't open my eyes until I felt him get off the couch.

Slowly then, I sat up and said abruptly without looking at him, "I need to go back to the dorm."

"Sure, I'll take you back," he said with the tiniest tone of guilt – which I probably imagined.

Relieved that there was no argument, I prepared myself to sleep in the yew hedge in the courtyard of the dormitory if the night guard wouldn't allow me in. As it turned out, the guard didn't stop me or ask to see my ID as I passed through the door. He gave me a suggestive smile. Was my hair messy? Were my clothes rumpled? Did I look "easy"? I scowled at him as I passed. He looked away and said nothing. Maybe he feared what I would do if he stopped me. Did I look homicidal? I certainly felt so. If I had a gun, I might have used it, but neither on the guard nor on myself...

Up in my room I locked the door behind me. Questions screamed inside my head. What should I have done? Did I flirt? Did I give the wrong impression? Whatever possessed me to drink so much? Whatever possessed me to go out with Norm? Why didn't I go home for Christmas? What should I do now? I told no one what happened, but a person can't endure, without release, the intensity of the anger and shame that now built inside me.

So, I ate like a starving person. For weeks and weeks and weeks. And meanwhile I read self-help books, such as Dad's Dale Carnegie book, and *I'm OK – You're OK* by Thomas A. Harris, to name a couple. What typically happened when I read these books is that I fell asleep and spilled food on the pages. I can't say I absorbed much of what I read.

At the end of Spring Quarter in 1972, I moved out of the dorm. I had no diploma, and no idea what I wanted to do with my life. All I knew was that I wanted out. Temporarily I moved in with some of my college friends who rented an apartment a few blocks from the dorm. I took a full-time clerk job at the Minnesota Department of Health where I worked until I heard that the manager of the Latin American Sales Division at Doboy in New Richmond, Wisconsin was looking for a Spanish speaking secretary. I applied and was hired. Sometime before I left Minneapolis there was a family event at Uncle Willis' house. One of my aunts was in town, I think. I attended with trepidation. I hadn't been there since before the assault. Would Norm be there?

I entered Uncle Willis' living room through the open front door. Comradely voices came from the kitchen where the Erions always gathered around Uncle Willis' round wooden table. I would have joined them except I recognized one of the voices was Norman's. For a few minutes I skulked in the living room like a guilty offender. Then Norm came in from the kitchen, passing through on his way to the front door.

No "Hello" or "Nice to see you" as he strode quickly past me toward the door.

What he tossed at me with a scoff as he went by was, "You've gotten fat!" Yes, I had, but that spiteful jab didn't merit a response. To myself only I said … and you're slimier than ever! I put on my "everything's fine" face and went into the kitchen.

~

Heinz

When a man loves a woman
Down deep in his soul
She can bring him such misery
If she plays him for a fool
He's the last one to know
Loving eyes can't ever see

From *When A Man Loves A Woman* by Andrew
James Wright and Calvin Houston Lewis

I met Heinz at a small party in a friend's home just south of New Richmond. The party was thrown by a former student of his who worked with me at Doboy. Heinz had been her German teacher. He was a happy-looking, blonde, blue-eyed man with shoulders like a linebacker. His youthful voice and enthusiasm belied the eleven years he had on me.

My latent bully awakened. I had been to South America. I, who hadn't managed to graduate from college, would make short work of this small-town boy who thought he could teach German because he had probably spent one summer at German Camp in northern Minnesota.

"Have you ever been to Germany?" I asked in a patronizing tone.

"I was born there."

I didn't see that coming. His perfect English gave no hint of German heritage. Absolutely no dialect. He spoke like a native Wisconsinite. Indeed, he had been born in the portentous year of 1939, the year Hitler invaded Poland, in what eventually became East Germany.

At the age of 40, the age of the fathers of many servicemen, Heinz' dad was ripped away from his family and conscripted into the German army. Der Fuhrer needed every able-bodied man. While Albert was gone Russian soldiers invaded the region, claimed the family farm, and killed and ate the livestock. Heinz and his mother ran for their lives but were captured by the Russians. They were put to work digging graves. It was the little boy's job to cover the graves with cedar boughs. For the rest of his life he had an aversion to the scent of cedar.

When the war was over Heinz' parents were able to locate each other with the help of the Red Cross. Although the boy could go to the west side of the newly established barrier down the middle of the country to be with his father, the Russians would not release Heinz' mom from the prison camp to go with him. One night she sneaked across the border, which was casually guarded in the early days. She hiked north for days until she reached Hamburg where she reunited with her son and husband.

The family assessed their options. There would be no returning to their farm now far behind the Iron Curtain. Factories on both sides of the divided country were piles of rubble. Undetonated mines were buried in fields. There was so little livestock that American mission groups, including one for which my Grandpa Stern volunteered, sent any animals that could be spared to Europe. To ensure their beloved son, their only child, would have a future, the Rudau family boarded a ship in Hamburg and sailed for the United States.

When they eventually made their way to Wisconsin, none of them could speak English. Heinz had to learn fast, or the American kids would beat up the little "Nazi". Heinz had seen enough fear and suffering to fill his heart with compassion for eternity. Instinctively, I felt that. Before I knew I was seeking refuge I found it in this man's embrace.

After a jolly summer of scuba diving in western Wisconsin lakes, canoeing the Apple River, and trips to Medford, WI to visit Heinz' parents, I took Heinz home to Spring Valley to meet my folks. Mom took the opportunity to put me into perspective for him.

"It's nice to see Kathy has a sweetheart," she said with a devious smile. "She never dated in high school. No one ever asked her out."

Speechless I stared at the two of them. Heinz looked awkward. Mom looked triumphant. I tried out various sarcastic responses – but only in my imagination.

"Don't get your expectations up, Heinz. I'm not much of a catch."

"I had to have my trysts during study hall because my suitors didn't want to meet my folks."

Regardless of imaginary retorts it was now abundantly obvious that my mother was not my advocate.

~

Dowry

I'd like to teach the world to sing
In perfect harmony

From *I'd Like to Teach the World to Sing* by William Backer,
Roger Cook, Roquel Davis and Roger Greenaway

When Mom and Dad moved to Cass Lake, I inherited the piano. What do you say to your parents when they bequeath a 500-pound millstone on you? I said something to show my earnest appreciation of their good intentions.

"Give it to Carlyn. You owe her a piano."

"This one is yours," said Mom, as if any day Carlyn would be in possession of a grand piano.

"But I don't have a place for a piano," I protested.

I could swear she answered, "Achtung! You vil take it und you vil enchoy it!"

Whatever her actual words she emphasized them with sparks that snapped from her eyes. Dad said nothing.

In my mind I gave a Nazi salute and replied "Heil Muttie!"

It was easier to move the piano than to stand up to her.

Grunting and swearing all the way, Heinz and two of his buddies heaved the piano from the bed of a pickup truck up a steep, narrow flight of stairs to my second-floor apartment in New Richmond.

I did sit down to play the piano once while I lived there. Within five minutes two elderly women emerged from their apartments and knocked on my apartment door.

"We heard the notes. How lovely!" they exclaimed. "We love to sing! We'll be over every time you play!"

That was the last time I played. The thought of embarrassing myself in front of an audience as I stumbled through a song book made me perspire.

~

Germany

Ich liebe die gros
Ich liebe die klein
Ich liebe die wie ein kleines schwein.

German Nursery Rhyme

In 1974 Heinz was selected as a Fulbright Exchange Teacher. He was off to West Germany for a year! In his first trip back to the Motherland since boyhood, Heinz would teach English to German high school students in the town of Holtzminden. He invited me to accompany him. I was breathless with excitement. Neuschwanstein, here I come!

We rented an apartment in a village called Höxter that was older than the United States. We ate schnitzel and drank German Pilsner until some well-intentioned soul introduced me to refreshing sweet Riesling.

One starless evening when darkness began to press down on the wan gray afternoon at the early hour of 4:30, we climbed into our teenagers' dream car, our secondhand chartreuse VW Kafer with black racing stripes along the sides and its engine in the trunk. We drove up to a theater in Holtzminden to see a movie starring the beautiful German actress Romy Schneider. Although I spent my days studying German as intently as I could, the language in the movie was too advanced for my ability. I stuck it out, but all I can tell you is that poor Romy died at the end.

As we left the theater the thick night air smelled so strongly of detergent that I wanted to gag.

"Can you smell that?" I asked Heinz.

"Smell what?"

"Laundry detergent. There must be a soap factory somewhere around here. I'll bet if it was daylight, you could see detergent particles floating in the air."

116

"I don't smell anything," he responded, lifting his nose to the nonexistent breeze.

"You really can't? The scent is so strong it's making me sick."

Heinz had a bereft look on his face that said women are inscrutable.

There seemed to be a lot of smells lately that made me want to retch. If I had felt that way only in the mornings, I might wonder if I were pregnant. But no. This had been happening recently at any odd time of the day or night, although nothing made me want to vomit more than Holtzminden's reeking detergent.

Actually, we had taken a home pregnancy test a few days prior. It was negative, but my period was overdue. It was time for a doctor's opinion.

Within days of the medical confirmation, we were on the rainy road to Amsterdam. Germany was a very Catholic country. The Netherlands was more liberal.

Heinz and I were in complete agreement that this pregnancy was not going to proceed. First was the fact that Heinz already had four children. In my mind, that was two families' worth of children. My allotment of children had already been born to another woman. I had read *Silent Spring*,[8] Rachel Carson's (Carson) treatise on human impact on our environment. There were three billion human beings on our planet when Ms. Carson wrote of her concerns in the early 60's. Seven decades later there are almost eight billion people vying for food, water and land on this same small planet, but back to the story.

Furthermore, my parents had made nothing as crystal clear to their daughters as the grievous shame of a pregnancy outside of marriage. A woman who was single and pregnant was as good as dead. Altruism be damned. It was me or the zygote. If I had loved that speck, that future human inside of me, the decision would have been difficult. But how could I love that potential life when I could not love my own?

The amiable, white-coated Dutch doctor went over the procedure with me as I sat in a cotton shift on the end of the cold metal examination table. When he brought up the subject of birth control, I asked what my options were to permanently prevent pregnancy. I listened indignantly to the gray-haired doctor explain in perfect English why he would advise against this for a woman of my age.

"You are so young. In a couple of years, you might very well have an entirely different attitude."

"No. I never intend to have children," I said tersely.

"Come back and have this conversation with me again in five years," he finished with a wave as he stepped out of the room to allow the nurse to prep me for the abortion.

I counseled myself that the doctor didn't know me. I wasn't the mothering type. What did people mean when they said children completed them, I wondered. That's a load to put on kids, isn't it?

Your job, Junior, is to make me feel complete. Fail, and you'll wish I had visited the abortion clinic.

On our drive back to West Germany there was no guilt, no remorse, no sorrow. Just relief. And for me one question: I wondered if I ever "completed" my parents. Probably, I decided. People are satisfied knowing they are smarter, wiser and more powerful than at least one other person on earth.

Later, I wrote this poem:

Motherhood
By Kate Erion

I don't feel kind or nice
Toward her.
I don't trust her.
She'll stab me in the back
At her first inconvenience.
It's hard to love Mother
Without trusting Mother.
Could I ever miss her birthday
And know she'll forgive me?

No!
Could I ever let Christmas go by without a gift,
And believe she'd not try to get even?
No!
Motherhood? Give me apple pie every time.

~

Re-Entry

"No trumpets sound when the important decisions of our
life are made. Destiny is made known silently."

Agnes DeMille

On the way back to the United States I asked Heinz what he thought about marriage. He wasn't a fan.

"Love hurts," was his basic sentiment.

"It's hard to watch another man move into your home, take your place with your wife, hear your kids call that guy 'Dad' while they call you by your first name. Meanwhile, you're sleeping on a buddy's couch."

Although I considered us a couple, I took Heinz' lukewarm attitude toward marriage as a "not going to happen" and made some one-sided assumptions about the constraints of our relationship, because I wasn't into being frank.

Back in Wisconsin I moved in with Laura my scuba diving friend who now owned a home in St. Croix Falls. I applied for a waitress job to support myself. The restaurant was a faded truck stop called Lee's on U.S. Highway 8. It was owned by a man who seemed to have cut his losses – as far as I knew all he had to care for was his livelihood. I did not know him well, but I never saw him with a wife or kids. Blue veins were visible in his large nose as he interviewed me in a booth at his restaurant.

Roger, the day cook with a red Yosemite Sam mustache above perfect teeth, interrupted us as he slid onto the bench on my side of the table.

"Hire her, Lee," he said.

"She's got the job if she wants it," Lee said.

Pressed between the wall and the cook's thick body I puzzled whether I should be flattered, offended or just darn grateful.

Roger

Selfishness – self-centeredness! That, we think, is the root of our troubles.

Alcoholics Anonymous

On weeknights when the influx of customers slowed down, Roger and I would sometimes find ourselves behind the restaurant taking a break together. We stood in the dark chatting and listening to passing highway traffic. When cars slowed down, we listened for the tires to crunch onto the gravel of the parking lot signaling our breaks were over. One conversation I recall from those chats is Roger, who was about my age, telling me he didn't know how to cook when he applied for the cook's job at Lee's. It's true that the fare was typically burgers and fries as opposed to haute cuisine, but a person still had to know to what temperature to heat the oil and how long to immerse the frozen fries. Moxie is the word that comes to mind when I think of taking a job for which one has no experience. Moxie is also the word I would use to describe Roger's sexuality. Roger was a married man, but that detail was irrelevant to his expressing his attraction to me. And his attraction to me was an irresistible elixir.

A couple of weeks after becoming co-workers Roger invited me to his home before our shift. I had a clear idea of what lay in store. I wasn't innocent. Afterward, Roger said he would be honest with his wife.

"It should go well. She will like you," was the essence he conveyed.

Roger must have been compellingly persuasive because I was invited back to meet his wife. And she did like me. And it was mutual. She was one of those unpretentious people you can be open with because she was forthright herself. For the life of me, I can't remember her name, but I can remember her friendliness, her acceptance, her frankness. She was not tall, not slim, not a physical beauty, but her heart was generous and open. If I had met her before I met Roger, she and I would have become friends on our own accord, although I can't say we would have become lovers. That would not have occurred to me, and I doubt if it would have occurred to her either. This was new for both of us.

The three of us sat in their tiny living room sipping Roger's home-brew which tasted more like hard cider than beer. The *2001 Space Odyssey* soundtrack played on their record player. When Roger suggested we all pile into their queen size bed together his wife encouraged me. Her lips on me were surprisingly stirring. She said the same thing about my lips on her.

Later as we lounged lazily in their queen-sized bed which spread literally wall to wall in their little bedroom, they suggested I move in with them. Driving home on rural Highway 8 toward St. Croix Falls that afternoon, I considered it. I had no long-term plans with Heinz, yet he was my rock. I trusted him like no other – after all, he had seen me without make-up. But we had not defined the terms of our relationship. Privately I felt entitled to do as I pleased, but I was wracked with guilt for keeping my afternoon proclivities secret. I told myself I would confess to Heinz as soon as I made up my mind what I was going to do.

Gaining on the Chevy ahead of me, I suddenly realized I'd be talking to Heinz sooner than I thought. That car ahead was his. He had taken a temporary teaching job in Turtle Lake when we returned from Germany. And school had just let out for the afternoon.

"Oh, shit, shit, shit!" I said to myself when his blinker went on and the vehicle veered onto the shoulder of the road.

I pulled off behind him.

~

Back to school

"Mistakes make you wiser, heartbreak makes you stronger, and wrong turns often take you to the right place. It all serves a purpose."

Quote from InspirationBoost.com

Heinz and I married in a modest ceremony that September, 1976. The very next day I enrolled in the Communicative Disorders curriculum at the University of Wisconsin – River Falls. While we were in Germany Heinz introduced me to a couple from New Richmond whom he had tutored before their move to Germany. The woman was a speech therapist in an American school in Germany. I could tell she loved her work by the way she talked about the kids.

"Sometimes when the youngest kids are really shy, I hold them on my lap while we work on their tasks," she told us with a beguiling smile. "Most of the sessions are one on one. I'm never in a classroom setting."

Was there anything less threatening than that? Decision made.

Every evening became a solitary study session – just me and my textbooks. Being highly distractible I closed myself alone in our upstairs bedroom. It wasn't that Heinz' hilarious spate of profanity intermingled with Willie Nelson's "Good Hearted Woman" funneling up the heat vents from the basement woodworking shop was offensive. It wasn't that cats sitting on class notes were troublesome. It was simply because my mind wandered from one thought to another as naturally as taking a breath. Again, and again, I had to wrench my focus back on the textbook while frustration mounted to exasperation. Finally, in 1980 with a giant exhale I graduated with a Master of Science.

After graduation I accepted a temporary job filling in for someone on maternity leave at the New Richmond Public Schools. I believed having a diploma inscribed with Master of Science meant I was an expert, so when at a loss for the proper course of treatment for a student, I felt inept and deficient.

You are supposed to know this, I accused myself.

I feared my ignorance was due to a hopeless intellectual insufficiency. I didn't realize that even people with diplomas ask for help now and then - ask for input from colleagues. As far as I could tell, people who revealed their vulnerabilities put themselves in jeopardy.

~

Pie

"Addiction is a relationship – a pathological relationship
in which obsession replaces people."

Patrick Carnes

The inexorable temptation of the pumpkin pie in the kitchen has me out of bed. I stand on a tread half-way down the unlit stairs. I can hear Heinz breathing while he sleeps in our upstairs bedroom. Downstairs the refrigerator purrs quietly. If I accept my Grandpa's God, I could say a prayer and return to bed. But I feel unbearable humiliation in supplication to his God.

"My way or the highway."

With only self-discipline as a defense, the pie wins every time. I do have remarkable resistance, nevertheless. I have been standing in the same spot on the stairs for twenty minutes. If I make a move, I know my feet will go down the steps, not up. Once in motion an uncontrollable force will take over. Thinking it, makes it happen, of course. I start down the stairs. It's peculiar, isn't it, that I don't mind asking the pie to save me, yet I resist pleading to God? I despise myself for my weakness while I revel in the delicate blend of pumpkin custard, nutmeg, cloves and cinnamon.

Goodbye Piano

"Well, I won't back down
No, I won't back down
You can stand me up at the gates of hell
But I won't back down."

Tom Petty

After the school year ended a position at the St. Croix County Health Center in New Richmond opened. The Adult Day Care needed a self-employed speech therapist to work with adults with mental disabilities. I grabbed the job.

Heinz and I bought an early twentieth century two-story house in town. The piano sat silent against a living room wall until a high school music teacher, who pitied the instrument, gave it a loving home.

It was good to have the piano out of our house because we pulled down plaster walls, sanded and refinished the solid Maple floor on the first level and installed new kitchen cupboards that Heinz built in his basement workshop. We replaced drafty windows with new ones. We hung wallpaper, remodeled a bathroom and added another. We built a deck off the upstairs master bedroom and a screened porch off the kitchen. Heinz built a clear-glass version of a stained-glass lamp by soldering pieces of glass together with lead channeling. The warmth of the lamp hanging low over the dining room table pulled us in like moths in the evenings.

Mom and Dad drove down from Cass Lake to spend a couple of days when the remodeling was nearing completion. I was excited for them to see the results of our efforts. Heinz showed Dad around his sawdust filled workshop while I gave Mom a tour of the rest of the house.

"That lamp's a dust-catcher," she pronounced gleefully when I showed her Heinz' handywork in the dining room.

I ignored her remark and continued the tour. Upstairs she reclined on our bed while I pointed out the wooden wall I had stained moss green to coordinate with the floral wallpaper I hung on the other three walls. It was her turn to ignore my remarks.

"There's a cobweb hanging from your wall sconce," she said as if cobwebs delighted her.

After supper that evening when we moved from the table to bask in front of the wood burning stove in the living room Mom's eyes suddenly popped. She whipped her head from side to side, then made a complete revolution in the center of the living room. With a cringe I realized what she looked for.

"Where's the piano?"

"I sold it."

"Sold it! You had no right to sell it! Val! We're leaving. Now!" she shouted.

Without a goodbye or good riddance, she huffed for the closet, yanked out her coat and stomped to the car. The car rolled down the driveway while Dad trotted across the snowy yard and flung open the passenger door. Curling his long legs, he cannon-balled into the moving vehicle just before it lurched onto the street.

Mom and Dad's Divorce

One of these mornings
That chain is goin'a break
But up until the-hen
I'm goin'a take all I can take

From *Chain of Fools* by Aretha Franklin and Don Covay

Around the age of 60 after suffering a life-long sleep disorder Mom was relieved to be diagnosed with narcolepsy. Her doctor prescribed Ritalin. A side effect the drug gave her was hallucinations. When Mom said she saw lights flashing in the woods Dad gave his own diagnosis of Mom.

"She's nuts!" he said without an ounce of concern or sympathy.

Dad didn't tolerate the quirks of others, humans or animals. I once witnessed Dad beat his new Gordon Setter puppy when it cowered and ran the first time Dad discharged his shotgun in the dog's company. Dad hadn't acclimated the dog with training guns prior to the blast. He abruptly labeled the dog defective and returned it to the breeder for a refund.

When Mom's hallucinations began Dad filed for divorce. Mom stayed in their lake home while Dad hit the road in his pick-up truck, sometimes sleeping in its bed under a topper.

It's impossible for me not to point out the irony that Mom had tolerated Dad's alcoholism, depression and related shenanigans for 40 years. However angry I was with some of Mom's behaviors, I thought she at least merited the "for better or for worse" vow, but then, who was I to judge?

After the divorce I asked her, "What are you going to do with yourself now?"

"I'm going to go back to college!" she announced with happy conviction.

"What a great idea! We can support that!" Heinz and I told her.

And we did. On holidays and her birthday, we gifted Mom tuition money paying it directly to Bemidji State University.

All progressed well until one of her professors expelled her from his botany class.

"He complained that I interrupted him too much," she explained to us, laughing. "He said I was a disruption in his classroom!"

"What did you do in his classroom?"

"I knew the names of trees and flowers he was teaching us about," she answered with pride.

"How is that a bad thing?" we asked.

"I guess he didn't like to be corrected during his lectures."

She said this with a smile and a head-tilt as if she was proud of her display of knowledge. Never mind the fact that she needed this science credit to graduate, a college degree could never take priority over limelight.

Heinz and I exchanged eyebrow lifts.

Ooh boy!

Al-Anon

Well, maybe there's a God above
But all I've ever learned from love
Was how to shoot somebody who outdrew ya
It's not a cry that you hear at night
It's not somebody who's seen the light
It's a cold and it's a broken Hallelujah

From *Hallelujah* by Leonard Cohen

As a working couple Heinz and I fell into a workday routine. After supper we would open wide the iron doors of our wood burning stove and settle down to enjoy a libation together. Heinz would drink a beer, and I would have a tumblerful – up to the rim - of Riesling. A wine glass doesn't hold much wine, even if it enhances the bouquet. Bouquet be damned, was my attitude. I wasn't sniffing the wine I was drinking it.

When one of Heinz' kids began using recreational chemicals, I went to the St. Croix County Health Center's chemical dependency unit for advice. The child in question was Heinz' oldest son, the one who at 14 rode his bicycle all the way from his mother's house in Circle Pines, Minnesota to Wisconsin before the Highway Patrol picked him up on the shoulder of the freeway and called Heinz. The boy moved in with us, and unintentionally challenged my paltry relationship skills. A chemical dependency counselor said little about Heinz' son. His advice was for me:

"Stop using wine as a sleep aid. As an adult child of an alcoholic your chances of becoming chemically dependent are high. Furthermore," he urged, "go to Al-Anon."

Whoa! In fear that I might become my dad, I swore off alcohol on the spot. I am nothing if not obedient. I began attending Al-Anon, where I found support for people who have a chemically dependent loved one.

New ideas began to expand my mind. Even without the spiritual principles of Al-Anon, which I fiercely disregarded, I managed to learn a few new things.

Both AA and Alanon use the same 12 steps. Step one is "We admitted we were powerless over alcohol – that our lives had become unmanageable," although in Al-Anon this step is often worded as *We admitted we were powerless over the alcoholic."* That step was indisputable, but I snubbed the other steps. They all recommended a faith in a Higher Power which was to me like believing in Santa Claus. However, Al-Anon members were sympathetic and shared useful advice to avoid the pitfalls of co-dependency, which I dutifully carried home as proxy for Heinz to employ with his son.

Al-Anon seemed to want me to say my own life was unmanageable. I did not see that having deep-seated feelings of inadequacy were symptoms of unmanageability. The way I saw it was either I had to try harder to be a perfect speech therapist who knew all the answers, or to accept that speech therapy wasn't the career I was meant to have. I finally concluded that before spending five years of my life pursuing a Communicative Disorders degree, I should have done more research. The career I was meant to have would certainly have made me happy. After a year of malcontent, I turned in my resignation at the County Health Center.

Then a boulder of depression slammed against me.

$\sim$

Mauve

You say I took the name in vain
I don't even know the name
But if I did, well really, what's it to ya?
There's a blaze of light in every word
It doesn't matter which you heard
The holy or the broken Hallelujah

From *Hallelujah* by Leonard Cohen

On an overcast chilly day in mid-winter I sat alone on the couch in the living room feeling purposeless. Nothing interested me. Nothing achievable, anyway. My tabby cat, tiny Mauve, strolled companionably into the room. She had just awakened and had eaten a snack.

Now she approached me as if to ask, "Anything happening?"

She stretched out her front legs sublimely and with a yawn attached her claws to the upholstery of the couch. As she pulled down with her claws her eyes half closed into comfortable slits.

"No!" I yelled as I brought my fist down as hard as I could on top of her head.

She collapsed on the bare floor and then gathered herself up and staggered away. In horror I watched her wobble into the dining room.

If I had understood I was depressed, I would have blamed nature for the clinical depression that made me malcontent. I most definitely did blame nurture and the behavior I had learned from my parents. But there was no denying it was my own clenched hand that hit Mauve. I jumped up and rushed after her.

"I'm sorry! I'm sorry! I'm so sorry!"

Albert

We're so sorry, Uncle Albert
We're so sorry if we caused you any pain
We're so sorry, Uncle Albert
But there's no one left at home, and I believe I'm gonna rain

From *Uncle Albert/Admiral Halsey* by Paul and Linda McCartney

In the late 1970s Heinz' mom died of cancer. A couple of years later Heinz' elderly dad contracted the Shingles virus. He still lived in Medford in north central Wisconsin where the family had moved from Germany in 1949. Albert was a teddy-bear of a man who spoke a unique mixture of English and a dialect of German called Low German. The two languages blended into a single language that was incomprehensible to English speakers and unintelligible to German speakers. Heinz was Albert's only translator. Medford was 100 miles east of us. There really was no discussion. Albert, who was an exceedingly social creature, was never meant to live alone. We brought him to live with us and he began to recover. Because Albert was undemanding the transition should have been seamless. The only problem was me. I was at such a low point in my unfocused life that I had no empathy or compassion for anyone who was not me. It embarrassed me to have Albert witness my lack of industry, my purposelessness. My response to that exposure was resentment.

Feral

"What does that mean – 'tame'?"
"It is an act too often neglected, said the fox. "It means to establish ties."

From *The Little Prince* by Antoine De Saint-Exupery

A panicked sparrow flutters against the windowpane inside the porch. I open the kitchen door intending to flush the bird toward the porch door and out into the back yard. Hearing the kitchen door open, the stray tom cat I have been feeding bounds up the steps from outside to greet me. It sees the bird and freezes for half a second. Before I can intervene, the cat coils its muscles and launches onto the bird, clamping it between its jaws. The fluttering stops abruptly. With a tight grip on the bird, the tabby scoots down the steps to the yard. Did I shriek at the cat's attack? The kitchen door opens and Albert steps onto the porch to see what has happened.

"Was ist los?"

I freeze for half a second. My muscles coil. I launch down the steps to the back yard like a feral creature.

Sue

I fell in to a burning ring of fire
I went down, down, down
And the flames went higher
And it burns, burns, burns
The ring of fire

From *Ring of Fire* by June Carter Cash and Merle Kilgore

During summers Heinz worked construction jobs. The summer of 1985 he had a job roofing a barn north of Star Prairie; a classic style white barn with wooden beams supporting a massive arched roof that peaked out over the second story sliding door on the front of the building.

"You should come out and see this farm," he enthused. "The owner has pastures full of goats and their kids. They are hilarious. And there are kittens rolling all over the floor of the barn."

The very next day I drove narrow rural roads past emerald pastures and rippled ponds to the farm. It was easy to find. Even in the 1980s curved-roofed barns were becoming scarce. And most of the existing barns housed Holsteins. There weren't a lot of barnyards with four-legged gymnasts spinning and leaping like Cirque De Sole acrobats. The funniest antics were when the kids used the adult goats as platforms and launching pads.

I was in the barn re-establishing my rapport with felines when the door opened, and a tall woman with short brown hair stepped inside. When I drove up, I hadn't seen anyone around except Heinz who waved from the roof.

"May I help you," she asked? Her smile was wide, telling me this act of trespass was not an egregious overstep.

"Oh, hello." I stood up and set a kitten on the straw-scattered floor. "Heinz told me about your cute critters."

She didn't look like she minded at all. Her eyes sparkled like she had just spotted the flavor of ice cream she wanted at a Baskin and Robbins counter.

"Who are you?"

"Oh! I'm Heinz' wife. You must be Sue."

We talked then about goats and their hijinks, and barns and their upkeep. She said I was welcome to come out anytime I wanted, and if she kept looking at me as if I were delicious, resistance would be futile. I wasn't looking for an affair. I thought that was something I would never do, that is to say, would never do again. It was just that being interesting to someone felt intoxicating.

Divorce

"We spend too much time looking for the right person
to love or finding fault with those we already love, when
instead we should be perfecting the love we give."

Author unknown

"Heinz, I'd like to go back to school," I said one solid gray day.

"Are you kidding me?"

"I'm thinking about getting a degree in journalism."

"Absolutely not! I felt like I was living with a crazy person while you were in school."

He had been, if you accept that depression is a mental illness. If only we had known.

But I blamed my querulousness on the closest person to me – outside of myself, of course.

"If Heinz would parent properly, I'd be happy."

"If Heinz would keep the back porch neat, I'd be happy."

"If Albert didn't have to live with us, I'd be happy."

Once I became convinced that Heinz was responsible for my unhappiness, I gave up on the relationship. Just like my education, I had chosen wrong.

To appease my vexation, I gave in to a new temptation: Sue's attention to me. Heinz was devastated. I refused to acknowledge my oversized role in the deterioration of the relationship. I moved out and filed for divorce.

I have a solid cherry trestle-style table in my potting shed. Heinz built this table. It was one of his first attempts at building furniture. In winter the tabletop shrinks, and a crack opens the length of the top. In summer the wood swells and the crack fuses. It breathes very slowly, one inhalation and one exhalation a year. Like an animal in hibernation. Heinz had employed all the skill to this table he had at that time. He did his best. And still the table cracked. Tender loving care can't fix all defects.

Sue and I ran our brief course of passion. At the end we came to individual but identical conclusions: I didn't like her much, and she wasn't crazy about me.

I lived in the ground floor of a two-story house in New Richmond that Heinz had converted into a duplex. It was mine after the divorce. Heinz kept our home. From the duplex I drove daily the 50 miles into St. Paul to work as a clerk typist at the Minnesota Department of Commerce. On weekdays I had no trouble getting up, but on weekends my legs might as well have been paralyzed. Late on a Saturday morning I laid in bed as the sun glowed brighter against the drawn shade of the bedroom's south window.

A memory came to me.

"I can't move my legs!" Robin screamed from one of the bottom bunks in the girls' dormitory at a South American YMCA.

Her blonde head looked still and comfortable against the white pillowcase, but her eyes were stricken with fear. Tears wet her cheeks. One of our traveling companions sprinted from the side of Robin's bunk to fetch Emilio, our chaperone. He dashed into our room, stooped his tall frame to avoid the upper bunk and whipped the covers back from Robin's legs. Her legs were lying straight, covered snugly to her ankles by her long nightgown, as if her body had been arranged by a fairy tale illustrator - or by a mortician. I watched as Emilio loosened the fabric pinned beneath Robin's legs and massaged her calves through her nightgown.

"Can you feel this?" he asked in a quiet, calm voice.

"I think so," she said.

Gently he bent one of her legs at the knee and laid it back down on the mattress. He picked up her other leg and repeated the movement.

Her eyes met mine and I turned away. If I knew nothing else at 19, I knew a person doesn't stare intrusively at another person's vulnerability. A couple of the other girls squatted close to Robin's bunk. Their voices were quiet. I went about the business of packing my suitcase in preparation for the day's travel homeward.

Soon Emilio had Robin sitting on the edge of her bunk. He held one of her hands and one of the girls had her other hand.

"Now try to stand," he said.

With their support she stood, and then she was shuffling toward the bathroom. She and one of the other girls went inside and closed the heavy wooden door. The rest of us stared at the door.

"She'll be alright," said Emilio, which is what we all wanted to hear, and she was.

I remembered that as I laid alone in my bed in the duplex. Had her nightgown pinched off her circulation? I never asked her about it. Asking personal questions always felt risky.

At this moment alone in my bed I wished for the comfort and support of friends who would gather around me and encourage me to move my legs; to stand up; to take on my fears.

Left to my own inertia I would still be in bed when the sun glowed against the western window shade. I pitied myself and my loneliness, but I had no solution for it. It was almost enough to make a person pray. Almost.

Loneliness finally trumped paralysis. I got up, dressed and drove all the way back to St. Paul. There was an Over-Eaters Anonymous meeting there in a church basement on Portland Avenue attended by misfits who welcomed me just as if I was one of them. Imagine! But none of them asked me whether I had accepted Jesus Christ as my Savior, so I tolerated them without putting up defenses.

Mom's Death

Whenever you're in trouble won't you stand by me
Oh now now stand by me
Oh stand by me, stand by me, stand by me

From *Stand By Me* by Aaron Joseph Neville and Charles Tindley

In our divorce Heinz had agreed to pay the current year's property taxes on the duplex, so I was angry when a county notice of overdue taxes arrived in my mailbox. I called Heinz to remind him of his agreement. My property taxes weren't at the top of his priority list, he excused himself, but he assured me he would take care of them.

"By the way, your mom called me a few days ago," he said.

"What did she want?"

"She asked me about the divorce … she wanted to know what happened."

I hadn't talked to her in weeks.

Surprised I asked, "What did you tell her?"

"I didn't tell her anything. I told her to talk to you."

Though relieved by his discretion I couldn't let go of Mom's inquiry. A call to offer sympathy to either of us, a call to listen or offer guidance also could have gone well. Never mind that I myself seldom offered sympathy to others, I chose to take offense at Mom's attempt to ferret out details I hadn't shared with her.

Often after Saturday OA meetings I would stay in St. Paul until evening to dance at Rumors, a gay bar on Robert Street. Whether or not I was gay wasn't something that I spent a lot of time deliberating. A therapist explained to me that we all fall somewhere on a continuum between straight and gay, with most of us falling somewhere in the middle of the spectrum. I had no philosophical difficulties with that. My impetus simply was to not be alone. Rumors offered a friendly solution for many a gay, lesbian or straight soul with nowhere else to go. One night in October 1986 I was on the dance floor enthusiastically singing "Hallelujah" to *It's Raining Men*" when a friend grabbed my arm.

"Melva's outside," she hollered into my ear. "She wants to talk to you."

"She can't come in?" I shouted back.

Melva Jean was Dad's eccentric first cousin, just ten years older than I. Her parents lived in Bemidji, a few short miles from Mom.

"She says you should go out to her. It's important."

I squeezed through the crowd to the back door and looked out into the chilly parking lot lighted by a solitary streetlamp in a neighboring lot. There was a dimly lit RV taking up more than its share of space in Rumors' tiny lot.

"She's in the RV," said my friend.

Curious, I stepped into the cold and crossed to the door of the RV.

"Melva?"

"Come in, Kate," I heard her croak from the rear of the RV.

I climbed up into the séance-like atmosphere where candle flames flickered.

"What's going on?" I asked, expecting to see a deck of Tarot cards fanned out on the table in front of her.

Melva's big-boned hands were clasped together on the table near a flickering votive candle.

"Sit down, Hon," she said indicating a single chair facing the table.

Tentatively I poised on the edge of the chair and waited for her to respond.

"Your mom died tonight," she said getting right to the point.

"What?!"

Adrenalin flooded through me.

"What happened?"

"She was at my folks' having dinner when she asked to lie down. She had some pain that she thought would go away if she could stretch out. That didn't help, so Dad talked her into letting him drive her to the Bemidji Hospital. They were in route in his pick-up when she apparently suffered a massive heart attack."

I felt my shoulders tense. I stood.

"I've got to get home," I said turning from the table.

"You're going home?"

I glanced back at Melva's bereft face. Was something expected of me? It never occurred to me that Melva might mourn Mom's passing, might need a hug.

"Thank you for letting me know," I remembered to say as I left her speechless still seated at the table.

The memorial service was south of Black Duck, MN at an unpretentious Mennonite Church that Mom occasionally attended. She said it reminded her of her family's simple Church of the Brethren. My sister and I each wrote some words about Mom for the service, but neither one of us felt we could get through our eulogies without our emotions spewing. A kind friend in my sister's horse owners circle, Dan, offered to read our words. Dan got up and walked quietly to the front of the unadorned nave crammed wall to wall with mourners. The size of the group was a testament to the feisty and earthy extrovert who was our mother.

Carlyn's writing was a touching testament from a protective daughter. Dan read her heart-felt words like they came from his own heart. Then he folded Carlyn's page and slipped it into his breast pocket. I expected him to retrieve my sheet of bitter truth from that pocket. I had chosen my words carefully and with as much fairness as I was capable of. I can't remember the precise words I selected, but I remember the resentment of the recalled abuse that always pervaded my attitude toward my mother.

Acrimony biased my mind. I put the entire blame for my unhappiness on Mom. If I had been the wise grown-up who would offer Mom the love and sympathy she needed, our relationship would have been at least 50% less fraught. I was years away from that realization. I wouldn't give her credit for her effort to be a good parent. Mom read to my sister and me when we were too little to read ourselves. She took us to church. She made sure we kept our dental appointments, doctor appointments and piano lessons. She took pride in putting meals on our table and keeping our clothes clean. Every Christmas the aroma of home-made cookies wafted from our kitchen. Every summer she took pride in the food she grew for us in her gardens. That I never felt her love was a subject for another time. The memorial service was a time for honoring what she did give us; for giving her credit for her efforts, but I couldn't let go of my grudges.

As Dan spoke his own words that bygones were to be bygones and injustices were to be forgiven, I wanted to leap out of the pew and scream at him, at everyone there: "I'm the victim here! Why does no one ever speak the truth about this woman?!" Dan wisely kept his eyes on the carpet as he spoke, and I wisely (or cowardly) avoided him after the service was over.

~

Another Way of Getting High

Baby, sweet baby, you're my drug
Come on and let me taste your stuff

From "Essence" by Mark Stephen Gardner, Sam Williams,
Hari Teah, Lawrence John Colbert and Jason King

I have to get up and go to work tomorrow, but here I am alone in the dark on New Richmond's grade school playground. I am 36 years old, but I pump the swing hard like an exhilarated kid until the whoosh of the descent makes my belly tickle. Euphoria! This is euphoria! Crazy. Yes, it is. Listen.

It's not about the swing. It's about the boy … the man, I correct myself. He's a man, even if he is ten years younger than I. He likes me. He must like me. This blonde man stops by my desk wearing his broad shoulders and slim hips. He invites me to lunch in his soft voice and his unpretentious manner.

Today I invited him to lunch, and he said yes. We walked up the sunny street to Rumors. No other patrons were there. It was too nice of a day. We had the pool table to ourselves. When he pulled back the cue a little gap formed between the buttons of his shirt. I had a glimpse of rusty-colored chest hair. As he leaned in for the shot, concentrating, his smile got a little bit devilish. He knew he was going to put the ball in the pocket, and he couldn't help himself from grinning.

This handsome man talks to me. Sometimes he talks to me about his wife, but I will not think about his wife tonight. Tonight, I will think only about his smile while I had him to myself today.

144

Nightmare

All the other kids with the pumped up kicks
You better run, better run, outrun my gun
All the other kids with the pumped up kicks
You better run, better run, faster than my bullet

From *Pumped Up Kicks* by Mark Foster

Although it's dark in here stark florescent light illuminates the big room outside. A path of ambient light directs the eye straight to this stall. He'll be able to see my feet! I tremble as I step up and balance on the horse-shoe-shaped toilet seat. I hold my breath to quiet myself. I realize I shouldn't have latched the stall door. All the other stall doors are ajar. This locked door is obvious. Trembling, I reach and push the cold metal bar back with my shaking hand and pull the door open ever so slightly. Its angle must match the angles of the other stall doors. The door must be still, as though it has sat open for hours ... as though no one raced in to hide behind it.

Through the crack on the hinged edge of the door I see a silhouette emerge in the doorway ... the black silhouette of a killer holding a rifle at an angle across the front of his body. He faces the bathroom. I see his head move slowly, reading the room from one end to the other, looking for feet. I stop breathing again.

I shake so hard I know he'll hear me! Don't move! Don't slip!

He steps into the room. He believes I'm in here! His boots scuff the tiles as he starts at the far end. I'm in the third stall from the other end. Wouldn't it have been too obvious to hide in the last stall? He pushes the metal door open and lets the light from the other room illuminate the space.

He moves to the next stall door, pushes it open. Works his way down the row. He's methodical. I have seconds left to live. There's no escape.

He reaches my stall door, pushes it. Face to face! Lifts his barrel. The blast explodes.

A paltry scream, no more than a gasp, really. My eyes pop open. I bolt upright. My heart pounds. I'm alive. In bed. So relieved. Where does a dream like that come from?!

~

Linda

Pretty woman, walking down the street
Pretty woman, the kind I like to meet

From *Pretty Woman* by Roy Orbison and Bill Dees

Clutching the phone number of the woman I had just chased down as she departed the lesbian singles' soiree, I sauntered back to my table through the crowd of New Year's Eve 1988 revelers. As I returned to the table, I noticed a new person. An athletic-looking woman wearing a long-sleeved red cable-knit sweater and tan jeans with the cuffs turned up to reveal red flannel lining was seated next to Amy, the friend I had come with to the party. This stranger was slim with curly shoulder-length brunette hair and stunning blue eyes.

"How do you know Amy?" I asked her.

"I don't know Amy." she said.

Hearing her name, Amy turned and looked at the stranger. The two exchanged indifferent glances. A new song began on the cd player. If my memory serves, it was the James Ray version of *I've got My Mind Set On You*. Amy stood up to dance with someone from another table.

"Would you like to dance?" I asked the new gal.

She pushed back from the table and stood up and up and up. The woman was 5'11", seven inches taller than me.

The music was too loud for talking. When the song ended, I motioned toward the front door. She was better dressed for Minnesota's December 31st temperatures than I was. I wore only a blouse and a wool skirt, but I was warm from dancing. A streetlight half a block down allowed us to get a serviceable look at each other, although I had to stand back a couple of feet from her to avoid getting a kink in my neck.

Later I tucked her phone number in my pocket along with the other phone numbers I collected that night. On New Year's Day, 1989, I tossed all but hers because I liked her answers as I interviewed her on the icy sidewalk:

"Linda Muhlenhardt," she answered. *Something a little more exotic - Lola? - would be fascinating … no … Muhlenhardt is exotic enough.*

"No, I don't drink." *Hallelujah!*

"I work for myself. I'm a CPA." *I have no idea what a CPA does, but hey! – She's employed!*

"About a pack a day." *No apology - a take me or leave me kind of girl.*

"A Pisces." *Water signs are compatible with earth signs.*

"One dog, a shepherd mix." *Crucial. She's an animal person.*

"No, I'm not currently seeing anyone." *Play it cool.*

"30." *Eight years younger! … But she is so darn cute!*

"Shakopee, Minnesota." *Small-town girl! Simpaticas!*

"Mankato State." *College-educated!*

Linda later confessed that she did have her mind set on me as soon as she saw me at the party. She said every time she planned to ask me to dance, I ran to speak to some other woman. I did not see her until she sat down at my eye level.

By April my duplex was sold, and I had moved in with Linda in Shakopee.

This is where the story would end if this were a fairy tale: They lived happily ever after. But this is not a fairy tale. Circumstances had changed, but I … not so much.

In our first year together, a number of normal life stressors occurred, and I mention this because I hadn't learned any new techniques for dealing with them. Eating and inviting romance were the only tools in my arsenal. I sold my house while Linda and I were still getting acquainted. Linda had her set way of home making and I had mine.

We discovered we were the antithesis of each other. A tip I had picked up from attending Overeaters Anonymous meetings was that avoiding sugar and refined flours would lessen the sensation of hunger and cravings. Another tip I learned from a stint in Weight Watchers was that vegetables are a food. Linda found my rigid evening menu hilarious: I only ate salad.

Meanwhile the willowy kid astonished me with her indulgence in Fiddle-Faddle, Butter Fingers and red licorice whips.

But they say that opposites attract. One of my favorite Linda lines is, "Together we make one complete person!"

About this time the newly established Minnesota State Lottery began hiring. On a tip from my boss at the State Department of Commerce, I applied and was lucky enough to be hired. Linda, too, made a job change. Just before we met, she quit a controller job for a Burnsville company that was going through staff changes. Shortly after I moved in with Linda, we moved her into her own private accounting office in Savage, Minnesota.

The most profound stressor, however, was when, six months after we met, Linda's dad Carl was diagnosed with pancreatic cancer.

I remember waking up alone in bed well after midnight one night. Peeking downstairs, I saw Linda illuminated in the living room by a single floor lamp. She was fully dressed in a too-pale yellow shirt and jeans because she had never come to bed. Seated on one end of the cool-blue couch with a lit cigarette in her hand she exhaled smoke into the silent room. Sitting so alone she was the epitome of desolation.

Carl was a quiet, hard-working farmer whom Linda adored. Her entire childhood she was his steadfast sidekick. When Linda was only six years old Carl fastened wood blocks to the gas, brake and clutch pedals in the old flat-bed truck he used in the hay fields. Carl and his hired men loaded the truck bed with newly baled hay while Linda drove this standard transmission vehicle slowly through the field. She steered by watching through the arch of the steering wheel.

Carl did not survive our first year. Dorothy, Linda's mom, was left alone on their farm outside of New Prague, Minnesota, twenty miles south of us. I anticipated what was coming and braced myself on the downslope of resistance, even though I knew this was the Universe's retaliation for my selfish attitude toward Albert. Linda was firm. Dorothy would move in with us. Dorothy had opinions. On everything. Dorothy expressed her opinions freely and continuously. Linda was amazing to me because she actually listened to her mother's non-stop one-sided conversation. Linda could repeat back later anything or everything her mother said.

The worst thing Linda would say about her mother's incessant talking was that listening tired her out. Subconsciously, a lesson began to seep in: listening shows respect. But I didn't absorb it all at once. In the beginning I took offense at what I considered domination by soliloquy. This woman talked more than my own mother. Without a shred of empathy for a new widow, I wrote an emotional vent letter to friends of mine – then, emotions diffused, threw the letter in the wastebasket without mailing it.

That evening Linda and I were nestled together on the basement couch watching television when we were interrupted by bumps on the second-level stairs that sounded very much like the noise of a suitcase being dragged down a staircase one step at a time.

"I have to see what that is," said Linda getting up.

The next thing I heard was Linda's pleading voice.

"No, Mom! At least stay the night. Don't head home in the dark. Let's talk about this in the morning."

I went upstairs where a distraught Dorothy stood beside her suitcase with my discarded letter in her hand. My stomach clenched as I watched Linda help Dorothy, now resolute, haul her luggage out to her car. All the way Linda begged her mother to reconsider, but to no avail.

Linda's concern for her mother and her grief for her father manifested itself in her anger at my "stupid letter".

What have I gotten myself into? I wondered.

I was ready to walk out then and there, but Linda said, "Not so fast. You promised if we had problems, you'd go to therapy with me!"

Damn! I had. So, we did. One of the most memorable things the therapist said to me was "If you leave this second committed relationship a pattern will be established: you enter a relationship; you encounter bumps; you leave the relationship. How many times are you willing to repeat that behavior?"

I considered those words. I prided myself as pledged to this liaison, but the therapist suggested I might not be seeing rightly. Furthermore, she prescribed for me a selective serotonin reuptake inhibitor, better known as Prozac. What?!

After a few weeks of therapy and a few weeks of Prozac I began to feel an unfamiliar sense of ease. Outside of taking the drug there was still more to be done that I was clueless to. I needed to learn relationship skills. In other words, the success of the relationship was not all on my partner. Huh?

The following summer on a warm Saturday Linda and I shoveled gravel into the rain-formed trenches along the sides of our sloping driveway. The objective was the prevention of erosion beneath the edges of the asphalt which would result in the crumbling of the tar. Our driveway is two football fields long and winds steeply through woods so thick no breeze can blow through. It was hot, humid work and neither of us was enjoying it. We were almost finished before we got into a shouting argument about my shoveling technique. I stomped up to the house leaving Linda to finish the work alone. That day I made a fateful and conscious decision.

I'm going to drink. People who drink have fun. I deserve fun! I told myself.

I remembered the warning the chemical dependency counselor had given me years before.

"As an adult child of an alcoholic your chances of becoming chemically dependent are high."

My logic?

He said "high", not 100%, so there's a chance I'll be fine. Besides, if I do become an alcoholic, I know what to do. I'll just go to AA.

⌒

Cancer

"I wish it need not have happened in my time," said Frodo. "So do I," said Gandalf, "and so do all who live to see such times. But that is not for them to decide. All we have to decide is what to do with the time that is given us."

From J.R.R. Tolkien, *The Fellowship of the Ring*

During the 1997 tax season Linda's wick burned at both ends. When her mom began complaining of a pain in her leg, Linda tried to drive down to New Prague to check on her as often as possible, but she couldn't free up her schedule to accompany Dorothy to a doctor's appointment. Linda asked me to fill-in.

Being Dorothy's chauffeur might have been awkward for the two of us, but in the intervening years Dorothy made an effort to say to me she was sorry we got off to a bad start. I give myself credit for having sense enough to take that as amends and agree with her, rather than to ask her why in the first place she would give credibility to something she took out of the trash.

Despite our improved relationship it was a surprise when Dorothy asked me to join her in the exam room to hear her test results. They shocked me. Her doctor hadn't found any source of the pain in her leg, but in regard to an afterthought request for an effective salve for a rash on her chest he said,

"I want you to see an oncologist right away."

The diagnosis was an aggressive type of cancer, inflammatory breast cancer. Fear stole Dorothy's words, and suddenly I wanted her to talk.

Linda now insisted to both her mom and me that Dorothy was going to live with us from that point on, and neither one of us argued. In 1999 the pain in Dorothy's leg was finally diagnosed as bone cancer, but it was the breast cancer that took her away before the Second Millennium.

Alcohol

"We don't choose to be addicted; what we choose is to deny our pain."

Unknown

As some might expect, my compulsive over-eating was overtaken by drinking alcohol. And with time my drinking increased from every weekend to every day. And every day I remembered my flip response to the worry that I might be becoming an alcoholic. Every day I told myself my alcohol consumption did not cause problems for me. I got myself to work every day, after all. And Linda, who could take or leave one beer a year wasn't bothered by my drinking. Did it matter that I neglected the care of my beloved gardens when I opened a bottle of Pino Grigio at noon on a Saturday? If I had been honest, the answer would have been "Yes!" but my deceptive brain said the study of wine (so refined a title for my proclivity!) was a fine replacement hobby.

Furthermore, I was sober when I drove … well, except those few times I drove home from wine tastings.

Sometimes I would test myself. I would go without drinking one night. When I was successful, the next day I would celebrate by opening a bottle of Merlot.

"You see? I can quit," and I toasted my will power!

On garbage day I would hold back some of the empty bottles so that the bottle count in the recycling crate wouldn't cause neighbors to talk. It never occurred to me that alcohol was increasing my self-consciousness. I guess having been self-conscious my entire life, self-consciousness did not feel like a problem.

In his later years Dad used to drunk-dial people. Sometimes he would misdial my number and be vexed when the person who answered the phone told the drunken caller to never call them again. When he did dial correctly, he would tell me confidentially that Linda had been very rude to him the last time he had called me, unaware that it wasn't Linda he spoke to.

"She told me to never call again!"

"Dad, you didn't call us. Linda never told you not to call us. You called a wrong number," I would say, but he was never convinced.

When I began to drink it didn't take long before I would open a bottle as soon as I got in the door from work. Before I changed my clothes; before I fed the pets; before supper. And while I was drinking and feeding pets and getting supper ready, I listened to the news. One evening there was a news story on TV about a Siberian Husky breeder/hoarder whose operation had been shut down. The unsocialized huskies needed new homes. Linda and I were Siberian Husky fans. When drinking is involved, emotions can become maudlin. After dinner I drunk-dialed a Siberian Husky owner we knew. He didn't answer, but I left an impassioned message in slurred speech that he should adopt one, or maybe two, of these pathetic dogs. I remember thinking I sounded a little drunk, but I doubted I sounded as drunk on the other end of the phone as I sounded to myself. The fellow never called me back. That's about the time I began to admit I was my father's daughter.

Change is hard even when a chemical doesn't own you. It often takes something catastrophic for a person to change. And in January 2004 an impactful catastrophe occurred. My boss, George Andersen, the first director of the Minnesota State Lottery was a decent guy, smart, funny, capable, honest – and the same age as me. It gave me something to contemplate that someone my own age was a father of two, had completed law school, had worked for the Pennsylvania Lottery and applied for the directorship of the Minnesota State Lottery when the agency began hiring. Upon acceptance of the job he moved his family to Minnesota from Pennsylvania. His accomplishments were not so remarkable that the earth stopped spinning, and yet it impressed me simply because he and I started our lives at the same time. He knew what he wanted to do, and he did it. Always comparing myself to others my age, I wondered if I had believed in myself like George believed in himself, what might I be doing. Did George, who was a big man, ever tell himself he was too fat to succeed, I wondered. I wished I knew where his self-confidence came from.

Late in 2003 someone complained that the Lottery could make more money for the State than it did if George wasn't so focused on pairing the Lottery's "fun" brand with the fun of bass fishing. Under George's auspices the Lottery sponsored a bass fishing tournament. Based on the complaint, the State's Legislative Auditor called for a performance audit on our agency. George was convinced he would be fired.

I walked into the Lottery foyer one Monday morning in January 2004. Jim and Charlie, two of our Lottery Security investigators, were standing on the balcony overlooking the front doors.

"There she is!" they said as they saw me.

These were the two comediennes who "baked" and frosted a foam rubber cake for me on the occasion of my agreeing to have coffee with them.

"We'll get the elevator for you," they called down to me, and just like that the doors glided open. When I got off on the second floor, they were both standing in front of the elevator. I waved to them and turned toward George's office. Jim or Charlie, I forget which one, took me by an elbow. What are these jokers up to now, I wondered. They escorted me to an empty conference room.

"OK, Wise Guys, what's going on?" I asked in bemusement when they closed the conference room door.

"Sit down," they said, pulling a chair away from the conference table and rolling it toward me. Obediently, I sat.

"George killed himself Saturday night" one of them announced without preamble.

"No, he didn't." I gave them dirty looks. What a horrible joke.

"Yes, he did."

"He's dead?" Could it be true?

"Yes."

"Oh God! I wonder if he had a heart attack!"

"No. He killed himself."

"Why would you say such a thing?!" I gave them both a scathing look.

They told me the bleak facts, the unbelievable truth. How in the world?! Why in the world?! What was he thinking?! What was he feeling?! Fear? Despair? Anger? How could such a smart guy not come up with a survivable solution to this audit!?

Before the day was over, it began to sink in that George's death would cause me to lose my job. I served at the pleasure of the Director. Every Director has the privilege of choosing her or his own assistant. By the time I got home that evening I realized I could not, and I vowed I would not, ever again drink so that I could manage to find a new job. I had to be mentally and emotionally fit for new employment. I did not open a bottle that night. I did not open a bottle the next night. By the third and fourth nights I told myself I was cured of the lust for alcohol. A cause to celebrate! Friday night I opened a bottle. Hey! It was a Friday night, after all! "Never again" had lasted four days. Sunday night I called the AA Intergroup office.

"I drink every night. I can't even stop drinking out of respect for my boss. Do you think I'm an alcoholic?" I asked the kind-voiced man who answered the phone.

The man listened quietly while I confessed my obsession. When he spoke, he didn't put a label on me or pass judgment.

"Has anything bad ever happened to you when you were drinking?" he asked gently, prodding my memory.

"You mean like a DWI?"

"Sure, or anything else."

"No," I answered, because I wasn't going to tell this stranger about a sexual assault I hadn't told anyone else about that happened thirty years earlier. "Does that mean I'm not an alcoholic?"

"I can't answer that," he said. "You could certainly learn more about alcoholism if you come to an AA meeting. You could learn enough to decide for yourself. You're welcome to attend any meeting, any time."

Going to an AA meeting suddenly felt like a huge step. I'd have to drink on it – I mean, think on it!

~

Alcoholics Anonymous

If your time to you
Is worth savin'
Then you better start swimmin'
Or you'll sink like a stone
For the times they are a-changin'.

From *The Times They Are A-Changin'*; lyrics by Bob Dylan

Three months later, on the morning of April 24th, 2004, to be precise, an imminent decision on my employment was expected to be handed down by the Minnesota State Lottery. Before I left for work, I phoned a friend who attended AA.

"Are you going to an AA meeting tonight?"

"Why do you ask?"

"It's time for me to join. I thought you might be willing to take me to a meeting."

"I'm not going to a meeting tonight, but you should strike while the iron is hot."

"I don't know where there are any meetings."

"Call the AA Intergroup number."

And that was that. The responsibility was returned to me.

PART III

Came to Believe ...

First Meeting

All your dreams are on their way
See how they shine
Oh, if you need a friend
I'm sailing right behind
Like a bridge over troubled water
I will ease your mind

From *Bridge Over Troubled Waters* by Simon and Garfunkel

It was five before the hour, and I still hadn't located the church that gave meeting space to the AA group. I was nervous enough to confess to a group of strangers my humiliating inability to control my drinking. Now as I drove my orange VW Bug back and forth on the streets parallel to the Minnesota River it was certain I would arrive late, putting a spotlight on the introduction that I wished to keep invisible.

In a desperate final attempt before I gave up and headed home, I called Linda's cell phone. Linda had gone to grade school in this community. She answered as she crossed the river on the Highway 101 bridge into downtown.

"I can't find the damn church!" I blurted.

"Where are you?" she asked.

"I don't know if I'm on a street or an avenue but I'm heading west. The meeting starts in five minutes, and I'm not going in there late!"

"What'll you do if you don't go to the meeting?"

"I'll go home and open a bottle!"

"You're kidding, right? … Hey! I just saw your car! Take a left on Holmes Street, go up three blocks and take a right. The church will be right there."

"You're a Godsend! Thank you! Thank you!"

Smokers were taking the last drags on their cigarettes when I pulled up to the curb. As they dropped their cigarette butts in the smokers' receptacle, I hurried to go in with them, just another caribou in the herd.

Blend in! At all costs, conceal your vulnerabilities, I coached myself.

But these smokers knew an unfamiliar face when they saw one.

"Here for AA?" one asked, holding the church's side door open for me.

"Mmm-hmm," I said with a slight nod.

"You're in the right place."

Should I be relieved that I was in the right place or be concerned that members recognized me as a newcomer?

I plunged into the first open chair I saw as I entered the basement social room. I took a breath and looked around the large room where two or three dozen men and women were seated at round tables. A few people looked, as Dad would say, "… like they'd been rode hard and put away wet", but most of them looked like an assortment of average, everyday people. Some like me were dressed in work clothes. Others were more casual. There were white-haired people, young people with tattoos and piercings, middle-aged people in their polo shirts and khakis.

Someone called the meeting to order. There was a great shuffling of feet and scraping of metal chairs as all stood to recite the Serenity Prayer in unison. That was followed by more shuffling and scraping while everyone re-seated themselves. I went along, trying very much to look like this was just another part of my normal daily routine.

I was thinking, "So far, so good," when the people began introducing themselves and naming their diagnoses, something like this:

"I'm Tom, alcoholic."

"My name is Dick, alcoholic and addict."

"Harry, a grateful, recovering alcoholic."

And then it was my turn.

Oh, shit, shit, shit! I said to myself.

Aloud I said, "I'm Kate; I don't know what I am."

A few heads turned to look at me while, blessedly, the people after me continued with their own introductions and pulled most eyes away from me.

The meeting got underway in traditional fashion with several readings, announcements and the passing of a donation basket.

Then the leader asked, "Are there any anniversaries to celebrate?"

A clean-cut young man I would have trusted to watch my purse stood up and walked to the front table. He took a coin out of a plastic sorting box and turned to face the group.

"I have a 24-Hour medallion for this woman here by the door," he said stepping toward me.

Had this wolf sensed my weakness, despite my best effort to appear composed? Though singled out and startled, a smile suddenly ignited my face. This guy might be a fellow caribou. I might be able to drop my pretenses.

The reckoning everyone suffers in making the decision to attend AA is acknowledged with a bronze coin about the size of a silver dollar. It is inscribed with the words "To Thine Own Self Be True", which in retrospect I found benign but curious compared to what I would have expected … something like: "No one comes to the Father except through me."[9] Part of the panic as I drove looking for the meeting was from knowing AA has a spiritual element, or, as I then put it, "a God thing". If I couldn't come to terms with "the God thing", I doubted that I could stop drinking.

The words on the medallion were the first inkling that however much AA might suggest a spiritual way of life, it is not a church nor is it under the auspices of a church. I appreciate that more and more as time goes by. A church tells its members what to believe. AA allows people to come to their own spiritual understanding.

A person seated next to me whom today I can't put a face on held open their palm and asked, "Do you want me to put a little mojo on that medallion for you?"

That person then passed the medallion on to the next person and so on until everyone in the room had touched – some might say "blessed" – my first medallion. It was powerful mojo. I haven't had a drink since.

And "The God Thing"? This is a mystery to me. Yet, trusting this ethereal "Higher Power" gives me assurance. It calms my fears. It helps me let go of things over which I have no control. The best definition I can offer is that allowing that there might be a "Higher Power" feels like a long-sought loving parent is looking out for me.

This trust came neither easily nor quickly. As I began to grow up emotionally, I was self-consciously guarded.

During the aftermath of one of the many mass shootings in our country, Linda made a condescending remark about another call for prayers instead of a call for gun legislation.

A little too defensively I revealed to her for the first time, "I pray."

"To whom?!" she asked, stunned.

"I don't know!"

I no longer trouble myself about defining "Higher Power". In fact, it's better that it's indefinable because the meaning flexes and changes for me as the years go by.

~

Dancing

I am the master of my fate
I am the captain of my soul

From Invictus by William Ernest Henley

Could professional dancer Derek Hough who rose to acclaim on *Dancing With the Stars*, be any more exquisite? His precision showed in his Paso Doble when he straightened to full height from the balls of his feet. As professional dancer Cheryl Burke arched her back cat-like and slid one leg sensually across the floor, I realized my own back was arched in reaction while I sat in front of the tv. Yes, I'm a *Dancing With the Stars* fan, but don't tell anyone. Critics are merciless. Cheesy is one adjective I've heard more than once. Yet this show entertains me. If it's not judge Bruno Tonioli's demonstrativeness or host Tom Bergeron's goofy jokes, it's the passion of the Argentine Tango or the romance of the Viennese Waltz.

As you might guess, from time to time over the years of watching DWTS I have asked myself how my life might have been different if I had studied dance. I can make a wonderful fantasy out of that dream, but little by little in the twelve-step program that is AA I have learned no matter what went before there comes a time when we all have to take responsibility for ourselves. A high school classmate told me in 2023, at the ripe age of 73, that she takes ballet lessons.

"Whaaat?!"

Since then, I joined the St. Paul Ballet's "Boomer Ballet" class. Sometimes I wobble. Sometimes I move in the wrong direction. Sometimes I have a moment of euphoria.

Enlightenment is gradual in AA, just like growing up. Because that is what happens in this organization. We recovering alcoholics begin to learn how to cope with life in mature ways we failed to learn, for whatever reasons, when we were young. We all hit red lights on our highways. We no longer pull over to the curb and turn off the ignition. Red lights aren't intended to end the trip. At lights we now stop and assess and prepare for the next block.

I now understand depression and self-doubt were my own issues to work through.

After my introduction to the Twelve Steps when I first joined Alanon, I wrote the following poem:

Rosetta Stone for Progress

I always thought

It was they,

Our husbands,

Our fathers –

Even our mothers,

Who were prejudiced,

Against a woman's potential,

Against a woman's adequacy,

Against a woman's ability to succeed,

But now

On my own

Confronted

By the world

I find

Prejudice

In an unexpected quarter –

Myself.

~

Sober Living

Parents can only give good advice or put them on the right path, but
the final forming of a person's character lies in their own hands.

Anne Frank

As I finished putting away our groceries my mind went to the next
chore on my list: dinner.

"Damn!"

I was supposed to have stopped on my way home from grocery shopping
to pick up our pre-ordered pizza. I cursed myself for my ditziness. Linda
had reminded me to get the pizza before I left the house that morning.

"Where are you going after the gym?" she quizzed me.

"Cub Foods."

"Where else?"

"Fresh Thyme."

"Where else?"

"Papa Murphy's."

"Good girl!"

After 30 years together her quizzes of me are justified ... useless, but
justified.

Apologizing to the dogs I put them back in their kennels where they
had spent their morning, and out the door I went.

Once in custody of the Canadian bacon, pineapple combo pizza I told
myself there was no reason to mention forgetting the pizza when Linda
got home from work.

But of course, as soon as Linda got home and stepped in our front door
she asked, "Did you get everything while you were shopping?"

"Yes."

"You remembered the pizza?"

Good grief, she must be hungry I thought as I answered, "No."

"You didn't get the pizza!?"

"I did get the pizza."

"You forgot the pizza after I reminded you!?"

"Yes."

"How could you forget the pizza!?"

"By being who I am," I said simply.

"But I went over it with you!"

"It's a good thing I'm cute," I said smiling.

"Geesh!" she continued venting, but she smiled then, too.

At that moment I had a realization: allowing exposure of one's vulnerabilities is freeing. One of the many side-effects of AA.

~

Epilogue

Dear Mom and Dad,

Resentments can last forever while we fixate on placing blame. I can hold you responsible for the origins of my depressed state of mind. You might blame your anger on your impoverished upbringings or injustices of the day. Your parents might wish my great grandparents had known better or dealt differently with their issues, and so on and so on until blame is laid on the very first Stern or Erion ever born. Then all of us can curse them. Would defining the source of our personal malaise make the following generations feel better? Doubtful, although knowing their histories might help us understand.

I recently found this note I had written on the bottom of a page in one of my daily devotional books: "It's hard to feel forgiveness for someone who doesn't feel the need to be forgiven." "Yes!" I said. But then I read in another devotional book something someone else wrote: "...our lack of self-love hinders our ability to love others ...". As my understanding expanded, my ability to love myself, then others began to grow. I must now love myself because I feel forgiveness of you.

Let's play time travel. Let's pretend the current me (the mature and still growing me that I am today, the person who has had the benefit of education and AA and therapy and Prozac and social philosophies that have changed over the decades) is your parent in your childhoods. You know what I would do with you to the best of my ability? I'd hug you tightly and often in my arms. I'd hold you on my lap and praise you frequently and encourage you again and again. I would hope to ask you about yourselves. I would ask you what your dreams are and what your favorite colors are. I'd make your favorite cakes for your birthdays. Every time I saw you do a good thing, a right thing, I would tell you how impressed I was by your behavior. And I hope I would listen to you. I hope I would pay attention.

I'm sorry it's too late to honor you with the respect you deserve. I must welcome opportunities to honor and respect people in the present. May this give you solace.

Rest in peace,
Your daughter, Kate

Bibliography

Stevenson, R. L. (n.d.). *A Child's Garden of Verses.*

Spock, D. B. (n.d.). *Baby and Childcare.*

Darwin, C. (n.d.). *Origin of the Species.*

The Holy Bible. (n.d.).

Blackburn, G. B. (n.d.). The Ballad of Davy Crockett [Recorded by T. E. Ford].

Meyer, M. L. (n.d.). *The White Earth Tragedy.*

Carnegie, D. (n.d.). *How to Win Friends and Influence People.*

Carson, R. (n.d.). *Silent Spring.*

The Holy Bible, (n.d.).

Printed in the United States
by Baker & Taylor Publisher Services